GOD
ISRAEL
and
BIBLE
PROPHECY

Levi Hazen

Unless otherwise noted, all Scripture quotations are taken from the Christian Standard Bible®, Copyright © 2017 by Holman Bible Publishers. Used by permission. Christian Standard Bible® and CSB® are federally registered trademarks of Holman Bible Publishers.

Scripture quotations in the afterword are taken from the (NASB®) New American Standard Bible®, Copyright © 1960, 1971, 1977, 1995 by The Lockman Foundation. Used by permission. All rights reserved. lockman.org

Collated and edited by Joyce Li.

ISBN: 978-1-87-867805-8

Lansing, IL
www.LifeinMessiah.org

Printed in the United States of America

Contents

Note to the Reader

The events of October 7, 2023, have once again placed God, Israel, and Bible prophecy at the top of our newsfeeds. On that dark day, over 1,200 innocent people were brutally murdered in an antisemitic rage while thousands of rockets were simultaneously fired at homes, schools, and hospitals. Two hundred and forty innocent people (children, women, and the elderly included!) were taken hostage, beaten, drugged, branded, and taken back to the hellish tunnels of a cult of death, also known as Hamas. The brutality of these horrifying attacks shocked the world.

Yet, for those of us who have spent time in Israel and know the history of the Jewish people, Hamas' demonic behavior was not surprising. Terribly wicked, but not surprising. Hamas has clearly stated and publicized their purposes in their charter, which can be found online with an easy search. Their stated goals include the destruction of the Jewish people and the state of Israel. Anyone familiar with Jewish history knows that when someone threatens the well-being of the Jewish community, the threat should be taken seriously and dealt with immediately.

So, where are Israel and the nations heading? Although we may not know all the details of the future, especially when it comes to the timing of the rapture, God *has* revealed a general path to us in His Word. Sadly, as I speak in churches across the United States, I have found a general resistance in most people to study large portions of their Bibles, namely the passages that teach about the future!

I suppose the reasons for this vary from person to person and from church to church. Some seem to evidence a type of false religious pride, whereby they think they are pleasing God by not having an opinion about Bible prophecy. Some seem to believe remaining ignorant about Bible prophecy elevates them to some sort of higher spiritual plane because they are "above that kind of thing."

No matter the reason, it is wrong. Bible prophecy should be read, meditated on, and studied just like any other portion of Scripture.

If you are interested in what the Bible teaches concerning the future of Israel and the nations, I pray this book will be of great help to you. Bible prophecy has blessed, encouraged, and grown me in my faith and understanding of the Bible. And perhaps you picked up this book just to see "what this guy is saying." I pray you would approach the Bible passages within this book with a soft and open heart, asking God to speak truth to you along the way.

Levi Hazen

Note: all the chapters can be found in podcast version at
www.LifeInMessiah.org/
thetovpodcast

Foreword

People want to know the future. They are intrigued by Bible prophecy, and specifically the role Jewish people play in the end of days. Unfortunately, most pastors today don't teach or preach on this subject. It may be that they mistakenly think the people in their congregations don't care about this subject or perhaps they don't feel confident about their own understanding of it. We still need to know the answers to questions about the role of Israel in biblical prophecy and also today.

Enter Levi Hazen, Executive Director of Life in Messiah International. Levi is a former student of mine who is unequaled in his passion for the Jewish people and what the Bible has to say about them. This book is unique in providing God's people with answers to questions about God's prophetic plan for Israel. What makes it so special?

First, Levi Hazen loves God's Word and has a holistic understanding of biblical prophecy. He understands both testaments and has a comprehensive knowledge of the Bible. This insight enables Levi to give us a book with a great overview of what the whole Bible has to say on this important subject.

Second, this book doesn't sensationalize Scripture. There are no hidden mysteries or secret numbers. It contains the plain exposition of Scripture, showing how the Bible speaks to our current situation. This is a vital necessity when studying the Bible.

Third, this book expresses God's great love and concern for His chosen people, Israel. Unfortunately, God's heart for Israel has too often been neglected by Bible teachers. Every page of this book communicates God's love for the people of Israel.

Get ready to read and study. Keep a highlighter and pen handy. Levi Hazen is about to open your mind and heart to the Bible, God, and a profound love for the people of Israel.

DR. MICHAEL RYDELNIK
Professor of Jewish Studies and Bible, Moody Bible Institute
Host and Bible Teacher on Moody Radio's Open Line with Dr. Michael Rydelnik

1

Why Study Bible Prophecy?

Some believers remain far removed from Bible prophecy. After all, they reason, weren't most of the prophecies in the Bible fulfilled thousands of years ago? And for those that remain, how can we know when they will begin to unfold?

Some may be keeping an eye on seismic events happening in the world today, speculating whether we are seeing Bible prophecies come to life in our own time. For others, Bible prophecy ranks fairly low on their list of concerns, and they don't understand "what the fuss is all about." Why worry so much about prophecy, some wonder, when things will eventually work out according to God's plan anyway?

No matter what attitude you hold toward Bible prophecy, if you are a believer, God's promises and warnings in Scripture are for you! From the time He created Adam and Eve, to when He dwelt with His people in the desert, to when He came in the flesh to deliver mankind through His death and resurrection, God has spoken to His creation, giving us promises and telling us what to expect in the future.

God has not only communicated future events to individuals in the Bible, but He has also preserved His Word through centuries of persecution and upheaval so it could be read and understood by each new generation. Because the whole Bible is the inspired Word of God, it's important to pay attention to all that's written in it—including the prophetic portions!

So, before we dive in for a closer look at key biblical passages about Israel, here are four reasons why studying Bible prophecy is so essential.

BIBLE PROPHECY IS ACCURATE

The Bible, as stated earlier, is the inspired, infallible Word of God. By infallible, we mean the Bible is completely trustworthy and accurate. One of the main ways we know the Bible is reliable is that a vast number of its prophecies have come to fruition. According to Dr. J. Barton Payne, who authored the *Encyclopedia of Biblical Prophecy*, there are over 30,000 verses in the whole Bible, and more than 8,300 of them are prophetic—that's 27 percent of all Scripture![1] The Bible contains 1,817 distinct predictions that cover a variety of topics, from the birth, life, and death of the Messiah to the rise and fall of rulers and dynasties. A number of these prophecies have already been fulfilled, while the rest await fulfillment in the future.

The Bible's track record for accuracy when it comes to prophetic predictions is unmatched among all the books ever written. If the Bible was fraught with predictions that were clearly untrue, we might have grounds to question its inerrancy and authority. However, as it stands, we can point to all the prophecies that were fulfilled in the past as being 100 percent accurate. This adds to our confidence that all the Bible's unfulfilled prophecies will come to pass exactly as foretold in Scripture.

Though God's faithful character is sufficient reason for us to trust in His Word, external evidence that corroborates what the Bible teaches can bolster our confidence by affirming the reliability of the Bible in tangible, fascinating ways. Here are a few examples, drawn from the book *Charts of Bible Prophecy* by

1   J. Barton Payne, *Encyclopedia of Biblical Prophecy: The Complete Guide to Scriptural Predictions and Their Fulfillment* (New York: Harper & Row, 1973), 674–5.

Dr. H. Wayne House and Dr. Randall Price, of Bible prophecies that were fulfilled historically and left archaeological evidence behind them.[2]

Jerusalem delivered from Assyrian siege under Sennacherib (2 Kings 19:32-33; 2 Chron. 32:1-23; Isa. 37:33-35)

During the time of King Hezekiah, Jerusalem was besieged by the army of Assyrian king Sennacherib. While the fate of Judah and the royal house of David seemed to hang in the balance, God sent a word of reassurance to Hezekiah through the prophet Isaiah: Jerusalem would be delivered from the Assyrian siege, and Sennacherib would withdraw and return to his own city.

We have archaeological confirmation of this miraculous deliverance in the Taylor Prism, a hexagonal clay prism unearthed from the ruins of Nineveh, the Assyrian capital. It records Sennacherib's boast of *laying siege* to Jerusalem in 701 BC but not the *capture* of the city, a victory that almost certainly would have been entered in the royal annals if it had actually happened. The Greek historian Herodotus records the retreat of the Assyrian army, and the assassination of Sennacherib is documented in the Babylonian Chronicle—a series of ancient tablets which provide an account of Babylonian history spanning several centuries.

All these records were discovered with the advent of archaeology, a fairly recent academic discipline established in the nineteenth century, and all of them originate from sources other than the Bible. Yet they confirm exactly what the biblical text has told us for millennia.

The capture of Tyre by Babylon and its sweeping, permanent destruction (Ezek. 26; 28:1-10; Zech. 9:3-4)

2   H. Wayne House and Randall Price, *Charts of Bible Prophecy* (Grand Rapids, MI: Zondervan, 2003), 17.

A prophecy recorded in both Ezekiel and Zechariah foretells that the city of Tyre, located on an island off the coast of modern Lebanon, would be captured by the Babylonians. The island would be made a bare rock, and the stones and timbers of the city would be thrown into the sea. Tyre would become a place where fishermen spread their nets, and it would never be rebuilt.

The historical fulfillment of this prophecy occurred when King Nebuchadnezzar, leading the Babylonian army, laid siege to Tyre from 585–572 BC. In 332 BC, Alexander the Great attacked Tyre, throwing the city's stones and timbers into the channel to build a causeway between the island and the mainland. Tyre was finally destroyed in AD 1291 in a battle between the Crusaders and the Muslim Mamluks.

The siege of Tyre by Nebuchadnezzar is detailed in the Babylonian Chronicles. The Greek historians Herodotus and Xenophon, as well as the Jewish historian Flavius Josephus, have also left records of these events.

The destruction of Nineveh by attackers with red shields and garments (Nah. 2; Zeph. 2:13-15)

The Bible also predicts the fall of Nineveh, the capital of Assyria, and specifies that the ones who would destroy the city would come clothed in red and bearing red shields. This prophecy was fulfilled in 612 BC, when Nineveh was captured by the Babylonians. The Babylonian Chronicles detail how a coalition of Babylon and Median armies, formed by Babylonian king Nabopolassar, advanced with red-colored tunics and shields to take the city. Nineveh was completely devastated by these joint armies, to such an extent that no one could remember where the city was located until it was rediscovered in the late eighteenth century and excavated decades later.

For those of us who already believe the Bible is God's authoritative Word, it shouldn't surprise us that the empirical evidence we have aligns with biblical accounts of what took place thousands of years ago. Though we ultimately trust the Bible to be true and accurate because of its divine Author, it's exciting to learn of historical and archaeological discoveries that affirm the reliability of His Word.

One of the ways we know God is God is because He foretells the future. Many people have guessed at the future, and guessed correctly, but how many have guessed hundreds of times about major historical events and been right with 100 percent accuracy every single time? This is something only God can do. As God states of Himself in Isaiah 42:9, "The past events have indeed happened. Now I declare new events; I announce them to you before they occur."

BIBLE PROPHECY PROVIDES COMFORT

A second reason why we should study Bible prophecy is that it provides comfort in the midst of sorrow. In 1 Thessalonians 4:13-18, Paul writes,

> We do not want you to be uninformed, brothers and sisters, concerning those who are asleep, so that you will not grieve like the rest, who have no hope. For if we believe that Jesus died and rose again, in the same way, through Jesus, God will bring with him those who have fallen asleep. For we say this to you by a word from the Lord: We who are still alive at the Lord's coming will certainly not precede those who have fallen asleep. For the Lord himself will descend from heaven with a shout, with the archangel's voice, and with the trumpet of God, and the dead in Christ will rise first. Then we who are still alive, who are left, will be caught up together with them in the clouds to meet the Lord in the air, and so we

will always be with the Lord. Therefore encourage one another with these words.

When going through a difficult trial, often we experience sadness and sorrow. In this passage, Paul is addressing the intense sorrow at the death of a loved one. Grief is a natural response when someone close to us passes away, but Paul writes that believers are not to grieve for other believers who have died in the same way as the rest of the world does: devoid of hope.

What is this hope the world lacks? It's the hope of a better life after death, the hope of being with the Lord after death, the hope of escaping judgment after death. In the above passage, Paul is prophesying about the rapture, when believers who have died will be resurrected and "caught up" together with believers who are still alive, to meet Jesus in the air and remain in His presence forever. We know death isn't the end, but rather the beginning of a glorious future where there will no longer be any pain, death, or sorrow.

So, how do we secure this glorious future? It's not by being good, performing charitable deeds, or donating money. We can't enter into God's presence by anything other than faith—faith in Jesus the Messiah. Our ticket into His future kingdom is a gift we can't pay for, because it's already been paid for us through the life, death, and resurrection of the Messiah. All we have to do to receive the gift of eternal life is to place our faith in the Gift Giver. Keeping our eye on what Scripture says about our future can help us find the comfort and encouragement we need to endure the trials we currently face.

BIBLE PROPHECY GROUNDS US

A third reason why we would do well to study Bible prophecy is because it presents us with a proper view of reality in our current age. We read in 2 Timothy 3:1-5,

But know this: Hard times will come in the last days. For people will be lovers of self, lovers of money, boastful, proud, demeaning, disobedient to parents, ungrateful, unholy, unloving, irreconcilable, slanderers, without self-control, brutal, without love for what is good, traitors, reckless, conceited, lovers of pleasure rather than lovers of God, holding to the form of godliness but denying its power. Avoid these people.

Paul was writing to Timothy to warn him of the difficult times that will come in the last days. Most theologians agree that the period known as "the last days" in the Bible began as soon as Jesus ascended into heaven. Which is to say, we've been living in the last days for quite some time! Though no one knows when the Lord will rapture the church, we do know that we are getting a little closer with every passing day.

As we continue living in the last days, one of the things we should guard against is false teaching, specifically coming from the "little-a antichrists" of whom John writes in 1 John 2:18-19:

Children, it is the last hour. And as you have heard that antichrist is coming, even now many antichrists have come. By this we know that it is the last hour. They went out from us, but they did not belong to us; for if they had belonged to us, they would have remained with us. However, they went out so that it might be made clear that none of them belongs to us.

We know in the future there will be a "capital-A Antichrist" who will exalt himself and even proclaim himself to be God. We are not at that day yet, or at least the Antichrist hasn't yet been revealed. However, we do have the spirit of the Antichrist among us, which is promoting false teaching on a continual basis. We need to be aware of the enemy's deception, and the best way to be aware of what is false is to be familiar with what is true. That's why it's so important that we have a daily discipline of reading God's Word. We need to display the same kind of wisdom as the Issacharites, "who understood the times and knew what Israel should do" (1 Chronicles 12:32).

BIBLE PROPHECY EVOKES LOVE

This brings us to the fourth reason why studying Bible prophecy is so important: it evokes in us a sincere love of God. We see this benefit of studying prophecy in 2 Timothy 4:8, where Paul writes, "There is reserved for me the crown of righteousness, which the Lord, the righteous Judge, will give me on that day, and not only to me, but to all those who have loved his appearing."

It may not be apparent at first, but here Paul is giving a prophecy about the future of the believer. Believers across the ages who have "loved his appearing" will gain a crown of righteousness when they stand before the judgment seat of Christ.[3] Knowing we will be judged before Messiah Jesus for heavenly rewards— not for condemnation—should evoke in us a sincere love of God that motivates us to live a more holy life.

We can expect trials of various kinds on this earth, but one day the promise of salvation we have received through Jesus will be fully realized. As Peter encourages the believers of his day in 1 Peter 1:8-9, "Though you have not seen him, you love him; though not seeing him now, you believe in him, and you rejoice with inexpressible and glorious joy."

Why is this so? "Because you are receiving the goal of your faith, the salvation of your souls."

3   This judgment will take place after the rapture of the church, but precede the establishment of the Messianic Kingdom. It is for New Testament believers only. The faithful who lived before Messiah Jesus are resurrected and rewarded after the return of the Lord. See Dr. Arnold G. Fruchtenbaum, *The Footsteps of the Messiah: A Study of the Sequence of Prophetic Events* (San Antonio, TX: Ariel Ministries, 2004), 755.

CONCLUSION

We have just covered four good reasons to study Bible prophecy (although many more could be listed!). First, Bible prophecy is accurate and a crucial part of God's Word. To neglect prophecy is akin to arbitrarily deciding what we want and don't want to hear from God. And that only harms us, our understanding of God, and our view of the world in which we currently live.

Second, when properly understood, prophetic Scripture comforts us. A biblical view of God allows us to experience comfort because we know He holds the future. Even when (not if!) we experience trials and heartache, we correctly understand nothing is going to thwart God's promises to restore us and the world.

Third, Bible prophecy grounds us in a biblical worldview. When our perspective on life is not in alignment with the Bible's teachings, we are prone to err in significant ways. Instead of being tossed around by strange doctrine, we want to be anchored to the truths of God's Word.

Fourth, studying Bible prophecy will yield a proper view of the future that will evoke a love of God and others within us. When we keep in mind our time on this earth is short and the return of the Lord is imminent, this will spur us to share the gospel with a greater sense of urgency. And when we hold to biblical teaching concerning Israel and the Jewish people, we have a right view of not only them, but also of God's unchanging character. Not only has God worked *through* Israel over the course of history, but He is at work *among* the house of Israel at this very moment, with great plans for their future restoration. It is to Paul's teaching on Israel that we now turn.

Listen to the episode for this chapter, "4 Reasons to Study Bible Prophecy," on The TŌV Podcast.

2

Not Abandoned

REPLACEMENT THEOLOGY—WHAT'S THAT?

Replacement theology is a doctrinal error that has persisted for nearly the entire duration of church history. Essentially, this doctrine teaches that Israel has been replaced by the church and no longer has a unique role in God's plan. Or, as defined by theologian Michael Vlach, replacement theology is "the view that *the NT Church is the new and/or true Israel that has forever superseded the nation Israel as the people of God.*"[4]

Unfortunately, replacement theology continues to be taught in most seminaries and churches today. This despite the reality that this view stands in contrast to nearly every passage that describes God's faithful character and covenantal relationship with the Jewish people. In this chapter, we will demonstrate why replacement theology does not align with the clear teaching of Scripture. Rather, it arises from two primary root causes Paul warned the church against in Romans 11: ignorance and arrogance.

Replacement theology has other names, including *supersessionism, inclusion theology*, and *fulfillment theology*. If you have never heard any of these terms, you may have encountered the view of replacement theology packaged or expressed in a different way. Rarely do people actually use the

4   Michael Vlach, *Has the Church Replaced Israel? A Theological Evaluation* (Nashville, TN: B&H Academic, 2010), 12.

phrase "replacement theology." More often, it is subtly weaved into a sermon or commentary and presented as established fact rather than an interpretive conclusion drawn from a non-literal hermeneutic.

The presumption that the church has replaced Israel is so widespread that most Christians have the idea baked into their thinking. For instance, have you ever heard it said, "All the promises God made to Israel have been fulfilled in Jesus"? Or, "All the promises to Israel are now fulfilled spiritually in the church"? Or, "The true Jews are those of us (Gentiles) who believe in Jesus"?

These statements, while they may sound spiritual, actually reflect the unbiblical view that Israel has been cast aside by God and replaced by the church. Not only does this wrong perspective ignore the clear, literal meaning of Scripture, but if you look at the outworking of this perspective over the course of nearly two thousand years of church history, you will see that replacement theology is not only erroneous but dangerous. For centuries, this doctrine has been one of the primary drivers of violent antisemitism perpetrated against Jewish people in the name of Jesus.

While church fathers like Justin Martyr, Origen, and Augustine have made incredibly valuable contributions to the Christian faith, replacement theology was sadly also a feature of their homiletics and teachings. Largely owing to the church fathers' influence, by the time the medieval period began, replacement theology had become widespread in the church. We must decide whether we will continue holding a doctrine that contradicts what the Bible teaches, even though it has been espoused by the church for such a long time.

Romans 11 is a crucial passage in this discussion. While replacement theology claims God has abandoned Israel in favor of the church, Paul categorically states in Romans 11 that God has *not* rejected Israel. A close examination of Romans 11 reveals God has established Israel for His unique purposes; they are chosen because of God's promises to the forefathers and He is planning to bring them into a restored relationship with Himself.

"ABSOLUTELY NOT!"

The book of Romans is addressed to a Christian audience in Rome. The church in Rome was composed of both Jewish and Gentile believers. Throughout the book, Paul switches between addressing all believers, Jewish believers, and Gentile believers (1:7; 11:12-24; 14:1–15:13).

In Romans 9–11, Paul spills a lot of ink as he seeks to convey proper teaching about the Jewish people, their standing before God, and the way(s) in which Gentiles should properly relate to them. One of the Spirit's main concerns, as He inspires Paul to write, is that Gentiles hold a proper view of Israel as it relates to God's covenant faithfulness. Let's examine a portion of Paul's teaching in Romans 11.

> [1] I ask, then, has God rejected his people? Absolutely not! For I too am an Israelite, a descendant of Abraham, from the tribe of Benjamin. [2] God has not rejected his people whom he foreknew. Or don't you know what the Scripture says in the passage about Elijah—how he pleads with God against Israel? [3] *Lord, they have killed your prophets and torn down your altars. I am the only one left, and they are trying to take my life!* [4] But what was God's answer to him? *I have left seven thousand for myself who have not bowed down to Baal.* [5] In the same way, then, there is also at the present time a remnant chosen by grace. [6] Now if by grace, then it is not by works; otherwise grace ceases to be grace.

Immediately, from verse 1, Paul addresses the question of whether God has rejected His people, Israel. The church had only been in existence for a few decades when Paul wrote Romans, but it's possible that some Roman believers were already tempted to think God had forsaken Israel. Their view of the Jewish people may have prompted Paul to challenge the misperception that God had really cast Israel aside. The answer he gives is emphatic: *Absolutely not!* Paul is Jewish by descent, and he is spiritually alive in the Jewish Messiah. He presents himself as living proof that God has not rejected the Jewish people.

In verse 2, Paul repeats himself for emphasis: "God has not rejected His people whom He foreknew." In other words, God chose or selected Israel in advance. Here, Paul affirms the Jewish people's current status of being chosen.

Paul then cites the story of Elijah as a biblical example of God preserving a faithful remnant for Himself. After God displayed His overwhelming power and gave all the prophets of Baal into Elijah's hand, Elijah received a murderous threat from Jezebel that sent him fleeing about 375 miles from Mount Carmel to Mount Horeb. Elijah, exhausted and afraid for his life, thought he was the only one left who served the God of Israel (1 Kings 19:10).

Paul then quotes God's word to Elijah in Romans 11:4. Basically, God said, "Elijah, you don't know everybody who's faithful to Me. Don't look at just your immediate circumstances and what you can see, but trust that I have a remnant of faithful Jewish people who have clung to Me." Paul applies Elijah's story to Israel's present reality: just as God preserved for Himself a remnant in Elijah's day, so a remnant remains today (v. 5).

Today, even though most Jewish people have not put their faith in Jesus as the Messiah, there are actually hundreds of thousands of Jewish believers in Jesus, spread out all across the globe! These Jewish believers are among the remnant that Paul writes of in this passage, and they are crucial to God's design for the church, which includes both Jewish and Gentile believers made one in the body of Messiah (see Ephesians 2).

This doesn't mean different ethnic groups lose their ethnicity when they join the family of faith, just as we don't lose our gender distinctions when we become followers of Jesus. Paul's point here is that God has preserved a remnant of Jewish believers "chosen by grace." This was true in Paul's day and continues through to the present time. All believers are saved by grace through faith, not by works, which Paul emphasizes in verse 6. This is the only way to salvation for all humanity.

ISRAEL'S STUMBLING AND GENTILE SALVATION

> [7] What then? Israel did not find what it was looking for, but the elect did find it. The rest were hardened, [8] as it is written,
>
> > *God gave them a spirit of stupor,*
> > *eyes that cannot see*
> > *and ears that cannot hear,*
> > *to this day.*
>
> [9] And David says,
>
> > *Let their table become a snare and a trap,*
> > *a pitfall and a retribution to them.*
> > [10] *Let their eyes be darkened so that they cannot see,*
> > *and their backs be bent continually.*

In these verses, Paul is describing the veil that lies over the hearts and minds of most Jewish people in the world today. This veil is keeping them from seeing Jesus the Messiah for who He really is, and the same veil covers the spiritual eyes of most Gentiles as well (2 Cor. 4:4). Since a remnant who have put their faith in Jesus exists, it's clear this veil has not prevented all Israel from coming to faith, but the vast majority of Jewish people are not yet in a saving relationship with their Messiah. One day, however, that will change. Paul continues,

> [11] I ask, then, have they stumbled so as to fall? Absolutely not! On the contrary, by their transgression, salvation has come to the Gentiles to make Israel jealous. [12] Now if their transgression brings riches for the world, and their failure riches for the Gentiles, how much more will their fullness bring!

The stumbling Paul talks about here refers to the initial rejection of Jesus by the leadership of Israel. Not all Jewish people rejected Jesus when He came to this earth two thousand years ago. We see throngs of people following Him: His disciples, the apostles, and the thousands of people who believed upon Him. Yet, while many Jewish people believed in Jesus during and immediately after His earthly ministry, the majority of the general populace and religious leaders rejected Jesus' claims of being the Messiah.

"Have they stumbled in order to fall?" Paul asks. In other words, are they "down for the count," disqualified from God's program? Did they stumble for no reason?

Again, *Absolutely not!* There was a reason for Israel's stumbling: because of the initial rejection of the Messiah by Israel's leadership, the good news of salvation has gone to the nations. We know God loves the whole world and desires everyone to be saved. But Paul gives us another specific reason why salvation has come to the Gentiles: to make Israel jealous.

For Gentile believers today, we need to be living in such a way that when Jewish people see Christians who worship the God of Israel, they would be provoked to jealousy—to desire the relationship with Him that we have.

Unfortunately, if we look at the relationship between Jewish people and Christians today, we see largely the opposite has occurred. Instead of drawing Jewish people toward Jesus, for the last two millennia, the church has been involved in major acts of antisemitism, sometimes theological and other times outright physically violent. The result is Jewish people often feel put off by even the mention of the name of Jesus. One of the main objections to the gospel I hear from members of the Jewish community is, "Why would I ever believe in *that man* who has caused so much harm to my people throughout the centuries?"[5]

This is an incredibly sad reality, one that we shouldn't attempt to defend or deny as members of the church. Instead, we should acknowledge the atrocities committed in Jesus' name against Jewish people, and express our deep regret and horror for the antisemitism Christians were responsible for throughout the centuries. Jesus loves the Jewish people and laid down His life for them, but He has been grievously misrepresented to the Jewish community.

So, instead of provoking our Jewish friends with hatred and disdain, Paul desires the Jewish people to be provoked with love and appreciation. The result will be that more Jewish people will desire to investigate Jesus and the New Testament.

In verse 12, Paul reminds his readers that Israel stumbled so the gospel of salvation could reach the Gentile nations. If the rest of the world received immense blessings from Israel's *rejection* of

---

5   Some Jewish people will not even mention the name of Jesus. Why? Because of the horrid persecution carried out against the Jewish people in His name. This reality is well-documented in books like *The Anguish of the Jews: Twenty-Three Centuries of Antisemitism* by Edward H. Flannery.

Jesus as the Messiah, imagine the even greater benefits that will come to the nations when Israel *accepts* Him as the Messiah!

In case we were wondering who Paul is addressing, he makes it very clear in verse 13:

> [13] Now I am speaking to you Gentiles. Insofar as I am an apostle to the Gentiles, I magnify my ministry, [14] if I might somehow make my own people jealous and save some of them. [15] For if their rejection brings reconciliation to the world, what will their acceptance mean but life from the dead? [16] Now if the firstfruits are holy, so is the whole batch. And if the root is holy, so are the branches.

Even though Paul was called to be an apostle to the Gentiles, his own people were constantly on his mind. He fervently desired to see his Jewish brothers and sisters come to faith in Jesus and made sharing the gospel with them a priority. As you read through the book of Acts, you'll notice that in each town Paul visits, he goes to the synagogue first to preach the good news to the Jewish people. This is in accordance with Romans 1:16: "For I am not ashamed of the gospel, because it is the power of God for salvation to everyone who believes, first to the Jew, and also to the Greek [or the Gentile]."

In Romans 11:15, Paul reiterates what he wrote earlier in verse 12. As the *Moody Bible Commentary* explains, "Paul was intensely burdened that the Jewish people come to Christ, for when they do, the world will erupt in spiritual vitality and life."[6]

Verse 16 informs us that because the patriarchs, represented by "the firstfruits" and "the root," were chosen and uniquely

---

6   Michael G. Vanlaningham, "Romans," in *The Moody Bible Commentary*, eds. Michael Rydelnik and Michael Vanlaningham (Chicago: Moody Publishers, 2014), 1763.

set apart (or made holy), the same is true for the rest of Israel, referred to symbolically as "the whole batch" and "the branches."

PAUL'S OLIVE TREE ILLUSTRATION EXPLAINED

Verse 17 continues with the theme of the branches and the olive tree:

> [17] Now if some of the branches were broken off, and you, though a wild olive branch, were grafted in among them and have come to share in the rich root of the cultivated olive tree, [18] do not boast that you are better than those branches. But if you do boast—you do not sustain the root, but the root sustains you. [19] Then you will say, "Branches were broken off so that I might be grafted in." [20] True enough; they were broken off because of unbelief, but you stand by faith. Do not be arrogant, but beware, [21] because if God did not spare the natural branches, he will not spare you either. [22] Therefore, consider God's kindness and severity: severity toward those who have fallen but God's kindness toward you—if you remain in his kindness. Otherwise you too will be cut off. [23] And even they, if they do not remain in unbelief, will be grafted in, because God has the power to graft them in again. [24] For if you were cut off from your native wild olive tree and against nature were grafted into a cultivated olive tree, how much more will these—the natural branches—be grafted into their own olive tree?

This passage contains Paul's olive tree illustration, which can be difficult to interpret because people often misunderstand what is being referred to by different elements of the tree. In order to correctly interpret this illustration, we need to remember Paul is still addressing Gentile believers (v. 13). So, when Paul says, "you, though a wild olive branch, were grafted in among [the natural branches]," the Gentiles are cast as the wild olive branch and the

Jewish people are represented by the natural branches of the "cultivated olive tree."

Below is a diagram of Paul's olive tree illustration. You may find it helpful to consult the diagram as you carefully read through Paul's illustration. Many people believe the olive tree is national Israel. But that is not the case. Paul teaches that the people of Israel (the physical descendants of Jacob[7]) relate to the olive tree in one of two ways: either as *natural branches of the olive tree* (Jewish believers), or *branches that have been cut off* (unbelieving Jewish people).

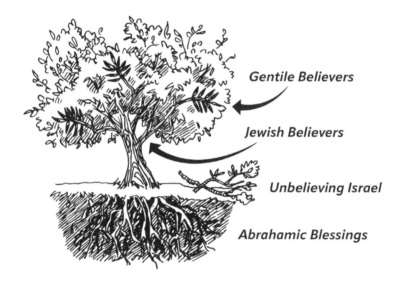

Gentile Believers

Jewish Believers

Unbelieving Israel

Abrahamic Blessings

This leads us to the question, "What does the cultivated olive tree symbolize?" One thing we can be sure of is that the tree is *not* Israel, because Israel is already represented by the natural branches, some of which have been broken off. If the olive tree were representative of Israel, this would imply that Jewish unbelievers—the broken branches (v. 20)—would cease being

7   God renames Jacob "Israel" in Genesis 32:28 and reaffirms his new name in 35:10.

ethnically Jewish because of their unbelief. Further, nowhere in Scripture do we find the idea of Gentile believers—the wild olive branches—being grafted into Israel. This would imply that believing Gentiles have now "become Israel," which reflects the erroneous beliefs of replacement theology.

Instead, in the passage, we see both some natural branches and some wild olive branches (Jewish and Gentile believers, respectively) sharing in "the rich root of the cultivated olive tree" (v. 17). The rich root and the cultivated olive tree are most likely representative of the blessings that emanate from the promises God made to the patriarchs. These promises include, among other items, a coming "seed" from Abraham—the promised Messiah. Jewish and Gentile believers partake of these spiritual blessings when they are in a right relationship with God through belief in Messiah Jesus.

Paul is still addressing Gentile believers in verse 18, warning them against arrogance toward the natural branches—the Jewish people. Many Christians, both past and present, have loved the Jewish people. Unfortunately, however, the majority of Christians have either been ignorant when it comes to the Jewish people or have displayed an attitude of superiority. But we need to heed Paul's warning in verse 20: "Do not be arrogant, but beware."

We are to beware because everyone is saved in the same way: by faith in Jesus the Messiah. God has provided no alternative path to salvation for anyone, Jewish or Gentile. Or, as Paul put it in Romans 2:11, "there is no favoritism with God."

Because salvation is by faith, when Jewish people turn from their unbelief, God has the power to graft them back into the olive tree again (Rom. 11:23). God's heart for the Jewish people is evident in this passage. He hasn't cast them aside or replaced them with the church. Rather, He desires that they come to faith just like everybody else.

In verse 24, we learn the Gentile "branches" were cut off from their native wild olive tree and grafted, contrary to their nature, into the cultivated olive tree. This is a fascinating picture of how God graciously extends His salvation to the nations. Gentiles originally had nothing to do with the Jewish faith. The God of Israel, the Hebrew Scriptures, and the need to believe in a Jewish Messiah were completely foreign to the nations (Eph. 2:12), with the exception of a few Gentiles who recognized Israel's God was the one and only God. Yet by God's grace, Gentiles get to partake of this faith that leads to salvation. We don't *overtake* it. We *partake* of it.

ALL ISRAEL WILL BE SAVED

Paul continues in Romans 11:25-27:

> [25] I don't want you to be ignorant of this mystery, brothers and sisters, so that you will not be conceited: A partial hardening has come upon Israel until the fullness of the Gentiles has come in. [26] And in this way all Israel will be saved, as it is written,
>
> > *The Deliverer will come from Zion;*
> > *he will turn godlessness away from Jacob.*
> > [27] *And this will be my covenant with them*
> > *when I take away their sins.*

Paul's use of "mystery" in verse 25 refers to something that was previously unknown in the Old Testament and revealed for the first time in the New Testament.[8] The mystery that Paul refers to here is likely the *way* in which God will save the Jewish people: through Gentiles who lovingly provoke them! This is also the

---

8   Vanlaningham, "Romans," 1764.

view of Dr. Walter Kaiser, who writes, "The mystery, then, is the process that God is employing to bring about Israel's final redemption."[9]

How great and mysterious is God's plan to employ believers from the nations to live in such a way as to draw unbelieving Jewish people unto Himself! Verse 25 reminds us that a faithful remnant of Israel who have trusted in Jesus for their salvation is a present reality. But when the full number of Gentile believers is satisfied, *all Israel will be saved*.

The *Moody Bible Commentary* calls verses 25-27 the climax of the entire unit of Romans 9–11. At a certain point in the future, all Israel will put their faith in Jesus their Messiah! No longer will a veil prevent them from recognizing Him, and no longer will their hearts be hardened against believing in Him. Instead, they will experience national regeneration.

But what does Paul mean by "all Israel"? Most likely, he is referring to the vast majority of Jewish people living at a specific time in the future, *not all Jewish people who have ever lived*. Any attempt to allegorically interpret "Israel" as the church in this verse also runs into significant problems—since all members of the church are already saved, why would Paul need to proclaim the future salvation of the entire church? Here, as elsewhere in Scripture, Israel should be understood literally as referring to the Jewish people.

Paul quotes two Old Testament passages that point to the Messiah's future deliverance of all Israel from their sins: Isaiah 59:20 (v. 26b) and Jeremiah 31:33-34 (v. 27). The covenant Paul mentions in Romans 11:27 is the New Covenant God made with Israel and Judah, recorded in Jeremiah 31. Through Jesus, Gentile

9   Darrell L. Bock and Mitch Glaser, eds., *To the Jew First: The Case for Jewish Evangelism in Scripture and History* (Grand Rapids, MI: Kregel Academic & Professional, 2008), 48.

believers are also partakers of the New Covenant, but we need to recognize that an integral part of this covenant is the national salvation of Israel.

> [28] Regarding the gospel, they are enemies for your advantage, but regarding election, they are loved because of the patriarchs, [29] since God's gracious gifts and calling are irrevocable. [30] As you once disobeyed God but now have received mercy through their disobedience, [31] so they too have now disobeyed, resulting in mercy to you, so that they also may now receive mercy. [32] For God has imprisoned all in disobedience so that he may have mercy on all.

Paul explains in verse 28 that many Jewish people, in rejecting the gospel, have become enemies of the gospel for the advantage of the Gentiles, who have been given the chance to receive salvation through Israel's stumbling. For this reason, Gentiles have no grounds for arrogance toward Israel. Paul also writes that Jewish people remain chosen and loved because of God's promises to the patriarchs. His "gracious gifts and calling"—the covenant promises made to Abraham, Isaac, Jacob, and their descendants—"are irrevocable" (v. 29).

God will never go back on the promises He made with the patriarchs and the Jewish people, and this should give us assurance as believers that God is faithful even when we are faithless. There is nothing Israel could do to make God revoke the covenant agreement He made with them and their forefathers. In the same way, as followers of Jesus, sealed by the Holy Spirit, we cannot do anything that would cause God to revoke His promise of eternal life to us.

Just as Gentiles once lived in disobedience but have received mercy through the disobedience of Israel, the majority of Israel has rejected the gospel, but one day their partial hardening will come to an end.

Conclusion

Replacement theology, then, is not just a matter of eschatology and what's coming in the future. To believe that God has replaced Israel with the church, or that He has permanently rejected Israel for their disobedience, is to call the faithfulness of God into question. In this chapter, we demonstrated why replacement theology, which stems from ignorance and arrogance, cannot be true in light of Paul's letter to the Romans. Now, we will transition to what *is* true about Israel and the Jewish people. This is best done by examining four major covenants in the Bible: the Abrahamic Covenant, the Mosaic Covenant, the Davidic Covenant, and the New Covenant.

> *Listen to the episode for this chapter, "Do the Gentiles Want to Know?" on The TŌV Podcast.*

3

The Abrahamic Covenant

Throughout history, God has chosen to govern creation and humanity through various covenants. A covenant is a contract or a binding agreement, and while some of the covenants recorded in the Bible were made between people, the major biblical covenants we'll look at in the following chapters involve God Himself as one of the responsible parties.

Each covenant God established is important, but one covenant in particular is crucial for us to understand if we are to have a biblical view of the people and the land of Israel. That covenant is the Abrahamic Covenant, found in Genesis 12, 15, and 17. This covenant provides a foundation for the rest of the Bible. If we forget (or neglect) God's eternal promises to Abraham, Isaac, and Jacob, we miss the importance of God's faithfulness and sow confusion where clarity is available to us.

The establishment and outworking of the Abrahamic Covenant highlights the reality that God's covenant faithfulness is never dependent on human obedience or disobedience. The same is true of other unconditional covenants in the Bible, such as the Davidic Covenant and the New Covenant (which we will cover in the next two chapters). These covenants, along with various ensuing covenants, flow out of the Abrahamic Covenant, which has provisions that can be organized into three categories: personal blessings to Abraham, national blessings to his descendants, and universal blessings for the whole world.

THE PROMISES OF THE COVENANT

In Genesis 15, Abraham—then known as Abram—asks God a question. How could he be sure he would possess the land God promised to him? In response, God tells Abram to gather several animals and slaughter them. It's a messy scene, with the divided animals laid out in two rows on the blood-soaked ground, birds of prey descending on the carcasses, and Abram shooing them away. As the sun sets over the Negev desert, God is about to establish one of the most important covenants ever made in history.

In order to understand how we got to this scene in Genesis 15, we need to go back a few chapters to Genesis 12, where God says to Abram,

> Go from your land,
> your relatives,
> and your father's house
> to the land that I will show you.
> I will make you into a great nation,
> I will bless you,
> I will make your name great,
> and you will be a blessing.
> I will bless those who bless you,
> I will curse anyone who treats you with contempt,
> and all the peoples on earth
> will be blessed through you. (vv. 1-3)

Notice the repetition of "I will" in the verses above. No conditional clause is found in God's promises to Abram. The fulfillment of God's "I will" statements are completely dependent on His faithfulness and character. God declared He would make Abram into a great nation, and He chose to carry out His promise through Isaac and Jacob, whose sons became the heads of the tribes of Israel.

God would also bless Abram. Throughout the biblical narrative, God provides Abram with abundant material possessions, protection from his enemies, and a son in his old age who would be his heir. Abram did nothing to deserve these blessings—in fact, the Bible records several instances where God blesses Abram *in spite of* his disobedience.

God also promises, "I will make your name great, and you will be a blessing." These promises are being fulfilled in the world today. Abraham's name is great not only among the Jewish people and adherents of Judaism, but among all nations because he stands as a major faith figure for at least three world religions: Judaism, Christianity, and Islam.

In spite of being the most persecuted people group on the planet, God has made the Jewish people a channel for His blessings to reach the nations. We see evidence of this in the outstanding accomplishments of many Jewish scholars in a variety of fields. As Michael Rydelnik observes, "The entire world recognizes the achievements of notables such as Jonas Salk, who developed the polio vaccine; Albert Einstein, whose theory of relativity catapulted the world into the atomic age; and Sigmund Freud, who is the father of psychotherapy."[10]

The number of Jewish people who have won international recognition for their scientific and academic work is truly remarkable. Among all the Nobel Prize winners in physics, for instance, fifty Jewish physicists account for 26 percent of the laureates! Undoubtedly, the achievements of these scholars are the product of years of hard work and dedication, but it would be a mistake to think their ethnicity is irrelevant to their success. In the Abrahamic Covenant, God clearly communicated His intent to make Abraham's descendants a blessing to the world.

10   Michael Rydelnik, *Understanding the Arab-Israeli Conflict: What the Headlines Haven't Told You* (Chicago: Moody Publishers, 2007), 125.

In other words, the ethnicity of the numerous Jewish men and women who have made vital contributions to science, medicine, technology, and other fields is not merely a coincidence![11]

Along with making the Jewish people a blessing, God also attaches a promise to this covenant concerning His response to the nations based on how they treat Abraham's descendants. Those who bless the Jewish people will be blessed, while the one who mistreats them will be cursed. Space doesn't permit us to go into detail, but there is a long list of nations that have tried to destroy the Jewish people over the last few millennia, and many of them are not with us today—at least not in their former state of power. In the rise and fall of nations throughout history, we see the active results of God's promise to Abram in Genesis 12.

God's final words to Abram in this passage are, "All the peoples on earth will be blessed through you." Greater than the blessing of medical and technological advancements pioneered by members of the Jewish community is the blessing of one particular offspring from Abraham's line—Jesus of Nazareth. Moses and the prophets wrote about Jesus, who fulfilled all the prophecies concerning the Messiah's first coming and will one day fulfill the remaining messianic prophecies at His return.

Genesis 12:5 tells us that Abram, in obedience to God, "took his wife, Sarai, his nephew Lot, all the possessions they had accumulated, and the people they had acquired in Haran, and they set out for the land of Canaan." When they arrived in Canaan, God appeared to Abram in Shechem, at the oak of Moreh, and reiterated His promise: "To your offspring I will give this land" (v. 7).

---

11   For further reading, see Jim Melnick, *Jewish Giftedness and World Redemption: The Calling of Israel* (Clarksville, MD: Messianic Jewish Publishers, 2017).

Throughout the rest of Abram's story, it seems as though Moses, the author of Genesis, is trying to emphasize that God's promises to Abram don't depend on his obedience or disobedience. Repeatedly, we read how Abram's decisions put the fulfillment of God's promises to him in jeopardy. At the end of chapter 12, Abram asks Sarai to deceive Pharaoh on his behalf, which leads to her temporarily becoming part of Pharaoh's harem. In chapter 13, Abram gives Lot the option to choose which part of the land he wants to settle on, which opens the possibility of Lot taking ownership of land included in God's promise to Abram.

In chapter 14, Abram goes to war against four kings in order to rescue his nephew Lot. God grants victory to Abram, and upon returning from battle, he meets the wonderful priest-king Melchizedek. Melchizedek, whose name in Hebrew means King of Righteousness, is likely a type (a foreshadowing) of the future Messiah or a preincarnate appearance of the Messiah. Though the Bible doesn't explicitly state who he is, Abram clearly sees this priest-king as a figure worthy of respect and reverence; he receives a blessing from Melchizedek and also gives him a tenth of everything.

This brings us to Genesis 15, which opens with a message of assurance from God to Abram: "Do not be afraid, Abram. I am your shield; your reward will be very great."

But Abram responds with a question. "Lord GOD, what can you give me, since I am childless and the heir of my house is Eliezer of Damascus?"

At this point, around ten years had passed since God first promised Abram he would be the father of a nation, yet Abram still had no children. In fact, another fifteen years would elapse before Abram's promised heir, Isaac, would be born. We may not like to admit it, but sometimes we get impatient if we have to wait several days before God answers a prayer. Imagine waiting for twenty-five *years*—and getting no answer! Understandably, Abram was growing despondent. "Look, you have given me no offspring," he says in verse 3, "so a slave born in my house will be my heir."

God responds by reassuring Abram that His words still hold true: "This one [referring to Eliezer of Damascus] will not be your heir; instead, one who comes from your own body will be your heir" (v. 4). Even though Abram had sinned, doubted, and disobeyed God, God's faithfulness to him was unchanged. In verse 5, God takes Abram outside and uses the stars of the sky as a celestial illustration of His promise. "Look at the sky and count the stars, if you are able to count them," He says to Abram. "Your offspring will be that numerous."

Abram was advanced in years, childless, and his wife was far past the age of childbearing. God's claim that his descendants would be as numerous as the stars may have sounded extraordinary to Abram (and to us if we were in his shoes!), but Abram responds with *belief*. He responds in faith, and it was credited to him as righteousness (v. 6). Despite the impossibility of Abram and Sarai conceiving in their advanced age, Abram trusts God will make good on His promise. No doubt this is a major reason why New Testament authors use Abram as an example of what it means to have faith (see Romans 4).

THE RATIFICATION OF THE COVENANT

In verse 7, God descends down to Abram's level to ratify the promise He already made to him. As the *Moody Bible Commentary* explains, "In ratifying the Abrahamic covenant God is not 'activating' it, but rather establishing the certainty of its fulfillment in the mind of Abram."[12] Not only did God want

12 Multiple Faculty Contributors, "Genesis," in *The Moody Bible Commentary*, eds. Michael Rydelnik and Michael Vanlaningham (Chicago: Moody Publishers, 2014), 72.

to solidify Abram's confidence in the promise, but His act would also affirm the faith of those who would come after Abram.

Beginning in verse 7, we read the following exchange between Abram and God:

> [God] also said to him, "I am the LORD who brought you from Ur of the Chaldeans to give you this land to possess."
>
> But he said, "Lord GOD, how can I know that I will possess it?"
>
> He said to him, "Bring me a three-year-old cow, a three-year-old female goat, a three-year-old ram, a turtledove, and a young pigeon."

The first thing we observe from this passage is the importance of the land that Abram and his descendants are given as a possession. Sometimes people minimize the importance of the physical land of Israel, or spiritualize it away, but since the Abrahamic Covenant was made without an expiration date (as we'll read later on), we can be sure the land of Israel has enduring significance in God's program.

We also see Abram ask God how he can *know* he will possess the land. In today's context, God's response to Abram's question probably puzzles us. Why does Abram need to assemble a small hobby farm in the middle of the desert? What does this have to do with his request for assurance concerning land ownership? To make sense of this passage, we need some background information on a particular custom in ancient Near Eastern culture.

When people in the ancient Near East were entering into a serious agreement or contract, it was customary to seal the agreement through a ceremony involving animal sacrifice. They would cut the animals in half, as Abram had done, and arrange the pieces opposite each other in such a way that it would be possible to pass between them. The parties making the covenant would then walk between these divided pieces, possibly grasping hands, and say something to the effect of, "If I break this covenant, may it be done to me as we've done to these animals."[13]

This is the solemn covenant-making ceremony God and Abram are about to perform in Genesis 15:10-12:

> So he brought all these to him, cut them in half, and laid the pieces opposite each other, but he did not cut the birds in half. Birds of prey came down on the carcasses, but Abram drove them away. As the sun was setting, a deep sleep came over Abram, and suddenly great terror and darkness descended on him.

Here we seem to have a problem. How is the covenant supposed to be ratified between God and Abram when Abram has fallen asleep? God has a solution, but first, He tells Abram,

> "Know this for certain: Your offspring will be resident aliens for four hundred years in a land that does not belong to them and will be enslaved and oppressed. However, I will judge the nation they serve, and afterward they will go out with many possessions. But you will go to your ancestors in peace and be buried at a good old age. In the fourth generation they will return here, for the iniquity of the Amorites has not yet reached its full measure." (vv. 13-16)

Ironically, part of God's answer to Abram's question about ownership of the land is that, for four hundred years, his descendants will be foreigners in a land that does *not* belong

---

13   Ibid., 73. This type of ceremony is also referenced in Jeremiah 34:18-20.

to them. God is foretelling the Egyptian bondage the Israelites would be subject to in the future, but He also promises their release from slavery in Egypt. The miraculous deliverance of Israel is recorded in the book of Exodus and commemorated annually during Passover, a major Jewish holiday.

Just as God promised, Abram died peacefully when he was 175 years old (Gen. 25:7-8.) Just four generations later, the sins of the Amorites reached their completion. God had given them time to repent, but they had refused. Their wickedness could no longer be tolerated. God used the Israelites to dispossess the Amorites, along with several other nations, from the land.

In verse 17, after the sun has gone down and Abram is asleep, God assumes the form of a smoking firepot and a flaming torch and passes between the divided animals *alone*.[14] This symbolizes God's commitment to take the full covenant responsibilities upon Himself. The animal pieces may have been burned up in the process, which would have prevented Abram from undoing what God had just done. The Abrahamic Covenant is unconditional because its fulfillment depends solely on God, who is perfectly faithful.

A central part of the Abrahamic Covenant is the land granted to Abram, whose borders God specifies in verses 18-21:

> On that day the LORD made a covenant with Abram, saying, "I give this land to your offspring, from the Brook of Egypt to the great river, the Euphrates River: the land of the Kenites, Kenizzites, Kadmonites, Hethites, Perizzites, Rephaim, Amorites, Canaanites, Girgashites, and Jebusites."

---

14   Multiple Faculty Contributors, "Genesis," 73.

The Brook of Egypt mentioned here is most likely not the Nile River but the Wadi El-Arish. It is located in the Sinai Desert, approximately thirty miles south of the Gaza Strip, and the riverbed is only full when it rains. This riverbed serves as the southern boundary of the land given to Abram. The Euphrates River, which marks the northeastern border of the land, is in modern-day Iraq.

Of course, the nation of Israel today is geographically much smaller than the land God promised to Abram and his descendants. Even at the height of David and Solomon's reign, Israel's borders didn't match the specifications of this land grant, and if they had, the land certainly hasn't been in Israel's permanent possession.

THE PERMANENCE OF THE COVENANT

Why is the permanence of Israel's land holding important? Along with its unconditional nature, the Abrahamic Covenant and all its provisions are also eternal. One day, in fulfillment of His covenantal promise, Israel will have possession of all the land included in the grant God gave to Abram and his descendants, and the land will be theirs forever. Isaiah describes this future scene in Isaiah 27:12-13:

> On that day
> the LORD will thresh grain from the Euphrates River
> as far as the Wadi of Egypt,
> and you Israelites will be gathered one by one.
> On that day
> a great ram's horn will be blown,
> and those lost in the land of Assyria will come,
> as well as those dispersed in the land of Egypt;
> and they will worship the LORD
> at Jerusalem on the holy mountain.

The eternal nature of the Abrahamic Covenant and the land promise included within it is also found in Genesis 13:14-15, where God tells Abram after he and Lot had separated, "Look from the place where you are. Look north and south, east and west, for I will give you and your offspring *forever* all the land that you see" (emphasis added).

The word "forever" in this verse is translated from the Hebrew word *olam*, but if we look at other places where the same word is used in Scripture, we see that *olam* doesn't always mean "for all eternity." For example, in Exodus 21:6, a slave who is permitted to go free but willingly chooses to continue serving his master will have his ear pierced against a door or doorpost, signifying that "he will serve his master for life." The Hebrew word translated "for life" is also *olam*, but here it means for the duration of the life of the slave, not for all eternity.

This raises the question of whether God's land grant to Israel was intended to be forever, or for a considerable but finite period of time. Looking at another biblical Hebrew phrase, *min olam v'ad olam*, can help resolve the issue. This phrase, according to Michael Rydelnik, is typically translated "forever and ever" or "from everlasting to everlasting," and it is "the strongest expression in Hebrew to describe perpetuity and eternality."[15]

When *min olam v'ad olam* is used in Scripture, it almost always pertains to God and His eternal nature. There are only two exceptions to this rule, and both times the phrase is used in reference to Israel's eternal possession of the land. These two uses appear in Jeremiah 7:7 and 25:5, which speak of land God gave the nation Israel and their ancestors "long ago and forever"—*min olam v'ad olam*. Rydelnik concludes, "Biblical Hebrew usage simply has no stronger way to indicate eternality. Thus, Jeremiah's words could not be any clearer. God has given

15 Rydelnik, *Understanding*, 156.

the land of Israel to the people of Israel as a perpetual and eternal inheritance."[16]

One question readers may have at this point is: How can the land of Israel belong to the Jewish people if other peoples, like the Caananites, were living there first? The answer to that question goes back to the creation story. Because God made the world and everything in it, He reserves the right to give any part of it, or all of it, to whomever He chooses (Acts 17:24-26). It was God's sovereign decision, and not the decision of the Jewish people, for Israel to possess a unique land in the Middle East with specific borders.[17]

The Abrahamic Covenant and the land promise haven't been fulfilled yet, but we can look forward to the day when Jesus will return and set up His kingdom. During the Messiah's thousand-year reign from Jerusalem, the whole earth will experience harmony, and Satan's imprisonment will ensure he has no influence in the world while his binding is in effect. It will be during this Messianic Kingdom, which prophets like Isaiah spoke about, that Israel's borders will finally encapsulate all the land included in God's covenant promise to Abram.

THE PROVISIONS OF THE COVENANT

The provisions of the Abrahamic Covenant are threefold: personal, national, and universal. The personal aspect of the covenant concerned Abram. His descendants would become a great nation, Israel, and they would have the promised land as an eternal possession. In Genesis 17, God changed Abram's name to Abraham to reflect his identity as the father of nations and kings. As noted above, Abraham is also considered a major faith figure in Judaism, Christianity, and Islam. In addition to a

16   Ibid.
17   See also Exodus 23:31 and Deuteronomy 32:8.

great name, he and his descendants have been a blessing to the world in numerous ways.

The national aspect of the covenant concerns Israel, which was to become a people as numerous as the stars of heaven. The Jewish people will one day permanently possess the entirety of the land God gave them, but this promise awaits a future fulfillment when Jesus returns and establishes the Messianic Kingdom.

The universal aspect of the covenant blessings apply not only to Israel, but extend to include the Gentiles as well. Gentiles would be blessed or cursed depending on their treatment of Israel. The physical blessings of the covenant are reserved for Israel, but through Jesus the Messiah, the seed of Abraham, Gentiles can receive the gift of salvation and other spiritual blessings that come with being "heirs according to the promise" (Gal. 3:29).[18]

CONCLUSION

The Abrahamic Covenant is the foundation of various major biblical covenants that arise later in the narrative of the Bible. It is also crucial for understanding Israel's past, present, and future in God's program. Believers who understand God's unconditional promises to Abraham and his descendants will view Israel and the Jewish people, not through a lens of judgment, but in light of His everlasting faithfulness to them.

Listen to the episode for this chapter,
"Genesis 15: The Abrahamic Covenant,"
on The TŌV Podcast.

18   This section on the personal, national, and universal provisions of the Abrahamic Covenant is adapted from Arnold Fruchtenbaum, "Eight Covenants of the Bible," Ariel Ministries, March 14, 2024, http://www.messianicassociation. org/ezine17-af.covenants.htm.

4

Distinctions Between the Old and New Covenants

Imagine walking into Best Buy tomorrow and purchasing a brand-new Apple computer. It has the latest operating system installed, along with a big screen, powerful speakers, and even a touch bar. You pay for your new computer and take it over to the Geek Squad—the employees at Best Buy who help customers with their tech needs. There, you make a request. You want the very first operating system Apple ever developed installed on your new computer.

Blank stares, laughter, and utter disbelief are the responses you get from the computer technicians. So, you explain yourself. You had recently read an article from the 1980s about how amazing this "new" operating system is. Since it was pioneered by Steve Jobs, a genius in the computer world, you feel you can't go wrong by having the 1984 version installed on your machine.

The Geek Squad hesitates, but against all odds, they comply with your request. You walk out of Best Buy with the latest Apple computer powered by oldest operating system.

Of course, this is a highly improbable scenario. Most of us engage with operating systems every day when we open our laptops or pick up our smartphones, and we know they have come a long way. Apple's first operating system certainly worked, and it was even revolutionary for its time, but it would fail to perform the functions we require of our modern computers. The systems that run our computers and phones today are far superior to the earliest operating systems released by Apple and other major tech companies.

Similarly, if we compare the Mosaic Covenant (or the "Old Covenant") and the New Covenant in Scripture, it's evident that the New Covenant is the far superior "operating system." In this chapter, we will explore the differences between the Mosaic Covenant and the New Covenant. What makes these two covenants unique? Who are the contracted parties in these covenants? And how does understanding these covenants inform our overall reading of the Bible?

THE MOSAIC COVENANT

The main text for the Mosaic Covenant is found in Exodus 19:

> In the third month from the very day the Israelites left the land of Egypt, they came to the Sinai Wilderness. They traveled from Rephidim, came to the Sinai Wilderness, and camped in the wilderness. Israel camped there in front of the mountain. (vv. 1-2)

After approximately three months, the Israelites had traveled from Egypt to Mount Sinai. In the following verses, we read how Moses ascends the mountain and receives a message from God to deliver to the people gathered below:

> Moses went up the mountain to God, and the LORD called to him from the mountain: "This is what you must say to the house of Jacob and explain to the Israelites: 'You have seen what I did to the Egyptians and how I carried you on eagles' wings and brought you to myself. Now if you will carefully listen to me and keep my covenant, you will be my own possession out of all the peoples, although the whole earth is mine, and you will be my kingdom of

priests and my holy nation.' These are the words that you are to say to the Israelites." (vv. 3-6)

Here, we see God's relationship to "the house of Jacob" is based on His promises to the patriarchs, as well as His miraculous deliverance of the Israelites from slavery in Egypt. The promises of the Abrahamic Covenant belong to Israel unconditionally, so the purpose of God giving Israel the law wasn't so they could *earn* the promises (since the promises were already theirs), but rather so they could *enjoy* the promises by avoiding sin.

> After Moses came back, he summoned the elders of the people and set before them all these words that the LORD had commanded him. Then all the people responded together, "We will do all that the LORD has spoken." So Moses brought the people's words back to the LORD. (vv. 7-8)

Notice, however, that God hasn't actually told the Israelites what to do yet! Even before they had received any of the commandments of the law, the Israelites had already pledged to obey "all that the LORD has spoken."

This agreement between God and the nation of Israel is only the initial installment of the Mosaic Covenant. As we continue reading the Hebrew Bible (the Old Testament), we see how God continues adding law after law, statute after statute, that the people must obey if they are going to uphold their part of the covenant. The Mosaic Covenant includes over six hundred commandments, ranging from dietary restrictions to appointed times and blood sacrifices, that govern the Israelite nation.

Though we won't go into the specifics of the Mosaic Covenant, we will cover some of its characteristics. First, we need to recognize that though the Mosaic Covenant is extensive, and it makes up a significant portion of the Hebrew Scriptures (from Exodus to Deuteronomy), it's not equivalent to the *entire* Hebrew Scriptures.

This can be confusing for those who are trying to understand the Bible, especially considering how we commonly refer to the Hebrew Scriptures as the Old Testament. Using the designation "Old Testament" for the Hebrew Scriptures can make all the books from Genesis to Malachi seem outdated, and therefore secondary and inferior. This is simply not the case.

In his letter to Timothy, Paul gave instructions about the continuing value and relevance of the Hebrew Bible, writing, "All Scripture is inspired by God and is profitable for teaching, for rebuking, for correcting, for training in righteousness" (2 Tim. 3:16). Only the Hebrew Bible existed when Paul penned those words under the inspiration of the Holy Spirit. Therefore, the Hebrew Bible definitely should not be treated as inferior to the New Testament. Both testaments are inspired, relevant, and valuable. Both should be studied, meditated on, and memorized.

The division of the Bible into "Old" and "New" Testaments may inadvertently confuse Bible readers. These names seem to imply that the Bible has just two covenants, an old covenant and a new covenant. While most Christians correctly believe we are in the New Covenant age, we often fail to account for the fact that the Hebrew Bible contains multiple covenants, not just one "old covenant."[19] Further, when the New Testament uses the term "old covenant," we need to keep in mind that this is a reference to the Mosaic Law specifically, not the entire Hebrew Bible.

Second, while some people may separate the Mosaic Law into three categories—civil, ceremonial, and moral—the Bible

---

19   For further information on the biblical covenants, a great resource is a study by Dr. Arnold Fruchtenbaum titled "The Eight Covenants of the Bible." A PDF of this study is available for free at https://www.ariel.org/resources/come-and-see/studies.

doesn't divide the law this way. Making these distinctions can be helpful when we're examining different aspects of the law, but they are all *moral* in essence because they were commanded by God. For those who lived during the era of the Mosaic Covenant, this meant that failing to perform a ceremonial function as the law commanded was ultimately a moral failure.

Third, we need to be mindful that the Mosaic Covenant is *conditional* in nature. This means that its fulfillment is dependent on the behavior of Israel. As such, the Mosaic Covenant is different from the Abrahamic Covenant (Genesis 15), the Davidic Covenant (2 Samuel 7), and the New Covenant (Jeremiah 31), which are all *unconditional*. Unconditional covenants are completely dependent upon God's faithfulness and will never be broken by human fickleness.

Sometimes the Mosaic Covenant gets a bad rap, but just because it's old doesn't mean it's bad. In fact, Paul writes in Romans 7:12 that "the law is holy, and the commandment is holy and just and good." The problem with the Mosaic Law is that it is insufficient to bring about the redemption that's needed for the forgiveness of sins.[20] Similar to the earliest operating system developed by Apple, the law is good and worked well for a time, but ultimately it is insufficient. The blood of bulls and goats could temporarily cover the people's sins, but it could never permanently take them away. As we learn in the New Covenant, this is something only the Messiah can accomplish.

THE NEW COVENANT

Our primary text for understanding the New Covenant from the Hebrew Scriptures is Jeremiah 31:31-37. Let's read the first part of this passage.

---

20   See Hebrews 10:4-11; Galatians 2:15-16; 3:11; Romans 10:4.

"Look, the days are coming"—this is the LORD's declaration—"when I will make a new covenant with the house of Israel and with the house of Judah. This one will not be like the covenant I made with their ancestors on the day I took them by the hand to lead them out of the land of Egypt—my covenant that they broke even though I am their master"—the LORD's declaration. "Instead, this is the covenant I will make with the house of Israel after those days"—the LORD's declaration. "I will put my teaching within them and write it on their hearts. I will be their God, and they will be my people. No longer will one teach his neighbor or his brother, saying, 'Know the LORD,' for they will all know me, from the least to the greatest of them"—this is the LORD's declaration. "For I will forgive their iniquity and never again remember their sin." (vv. 31-34)

One of the questions we set out to answer in this chapter is, "With whom are the covenants made?" We learned from Exodus 19 that the Mosaic Covenant was made with the nation of Israel, and the same is true of the New Covenant. In Jeremiah 31:31, God declares that He will make "a new covenant with the house of Israel and with the house of Judah."

In verse 32, God distinguishes between the forthcoming New Covenant and "the covenant I made with their ancestors on the day I took them by the hand to lead them out of the land of Egypt." This can only be the Mosaic Covenant, which the Israelites entered into while they were gathered at the foot of Mount Sinai, three months after God delivered them from Egypt. The New Covenant will be unlike the Mosaic Covenant, which the Israelites failed to uphold.

In contrast to the Mosaic Covenant, which was inscribed on stone tablets and expanded as God gave more laws to the

Israelites, the New Covenant wouldn't be written on stones but on the hearts of the Israelites. The internalization of this New Covenant will empower Israel, through the indwelling of the Holy Spirit, to obey God and enjoy the blessings of being His people.

Verse 34 contains a promise of the future national salvation of Israel. All Israel will know the Lord, from the least of the people to the greatest. Paul also looked forward to this day in Romans 11:26 when he wrote, "And in this way all Israel will be saved." In the New Covenant, God will deal with Israel's sin once and for all through the perfect sacrifice of His Son. Jesus paid the penalty for sin on the cross, making it possible for a righteous God to forgive Israel's iniquities—as well as the iniquities of Gentile believers who by His grace are partakers of the New Covenant.

It should be noted that Jeremiah delivered this message to the Jewish people when the nation was in a terrible predicament. A few centuries earlier, the Assyrian army had invaded the northern kingdom, Israel, demolished it, and exiled many of its inhabitants. During Jeremiah's time, the Babylonians were on Judah's doorstep, and God had revealed to Jeremiah that Jerusalem will be decimated by the Babylonians because of Israel's sin.

Dark days lay ahead, but as we see throughout Scripture, God often incorporates hope in the midst of judgment. And that's what we see in the following verses from Jeremiah 31:

"This is what the LORD says:

The one who gives the sun for light by day,
the fixed order of moon and stars for light by night,
who stirs up the sea and makes its waves roar—
the LORD of Armies is his name:
If this fixed order departs from before me—

> this is the LORD's declaration—
> only then will Israel's descendants cease
> to be a nation before me forever.

"This is what the LORD says:

> Only if the heavens above can be measured
> and the foundations of the earth below explored,
> will I reject all of Israel's descendants
> because of all they have done—
> this is the LORD's declaration." (vv. 35-37)

Here, God affirms His steadfast love and commitment to Israel. Only if the fixed order of the universe is disturbed, and only if the unfathomable heights and depths of creation are plumbed, will Israel cease being a distinct nation before Him. The survival of Israel is certain even in the midst of catastrophe, because God is faithful to preserve His chosen people.

The New Covenant is initiated by God and established with Israel, but by God's grace and through faith in the Messiah, Gentile believers can also experience the spiritual blessings of the New Covenant. This does not mean, however, that the church has replaced the Jewish people as the intended recipient of God's covenant blessings. Scripture is clear that one day Israel will receive all the promised spiritual *and physical* blessings, but not before they acknowledge their sin and turn to their Messiah for forgiveness. As the *Moody Bible Commentary* says, "The new covenant, made possible by the blood of Messiah, brought redemption to the world and will ultimately bring unique blessing to Israel."[21]

---

21   Charles Dyer and Eva Rydelnik, "Jeremiah," in *The Moody Bible Commentary*, eds. Michael Rydelnik and Michael Vanlaningham (Chicago: Moody Publishers, 2014), 1154-5.

Jeremiah prophesied about the coming of the New Covenant, but has it arrived? The New Testament tells us it has! We read in Matthew 26:26-28,

> As they were eating, Jesus took bread, blessed and broke it, gave it to the disciples, and said, "Take and eat it; this is my body." Then he took a cup, and after giving thanks, he gave it to them and said, "Drink from it, all of you. For this is my blood of the covenant, which is poured out for many for the forgiveness of sins."

Here, at the final Passover meal Jesus would eat with His disciples, He taught them about the arrival of the New Covenant. It was inaugurated by the shedding of Jesus' blood. Being God in the flesh, Jesus is the only one who has the authority to usher in this New Covenant.

DISTINCTIONS BETWEEN THE COVENANTS

The Mosaic Covenant and the New Covenant are similar in that they were both made between God and the nation of Israel, but how do they differ? The major difference between these covenants is the Mosaic Covenant is *conditional* while the New Covenant is *unconditional*. The Israelites would need to observe the commandments of the Mosaic Law if they were to enjoy the covenant blessings, but the New Covenant does not have an if-then clause. It is simply God's promise, predicated completely on His faithfulness. As we know from Jeremiah 31, there is nothing Israel can do to nullify their status as a chosen people before God.

The New Covenant is also superior to the Mosaic Covenant in several respects. First, it has a superior priesthood. The Levitical priesthood was responsible for administering the Mosaic Covenant, but this priesthood, like the covenant, ultimately proved insufficient. The full redemption of sinners is only possible through the New Covenant, which Jesus established by His blood. Hebrews 7 tells us that Jesus attained the office of high priest not based on genealogy, but in the order of Melchizedek, who "remains a priest forever" (v. 3). Jesus became a priest by oath, and His priesthood is permanent. These characteristics of Jesus' priestly ministry make the New Covenant priesthood more powerful, final, and effective than the Levitical priesthood.

Second, the New Covenant is also based on a better sacrifice. Under the Mosaic Law, priests needed to continually perform sacrifices to cover the sins of the people; the sacrifices had to be repeated because the blood of bulls and goats could not remove sins. With the New Covenant, however, there is a once-and-for-all sacrifice, that of the God-Man, Jesus of Nazareth. His blood is far superior to the blood of animals because it has the power to fully remove sins—past, present, and future.

CONCLUSION

With the arrival of the New Covenant, the Mosaic Covenant is completely outdated. It's an operating system that God no longer uses to govern Israel or the world. Installing the new operating system—the New Covenant—is a choice God graciously offers to each individual, and it doesn't involve a trip to the nearest Best Buy. All we need to do is believe in Jesus of Nazareth. When we put our faith in Him, we are born again (John 3:3)—that is, spiritually reborn. At that moment the Holy Spirit indwells us, establishing our "new operating system," and the process of sanctification begins as He begins to remake us in Messiah's image.

Listen to the episode for this chapter, "Old vs. New: Distinctions between the Covenants," on The TŌV Podcast.

5

The Davidic Covenant

In the previous two chapters, we covered three major covenants in the Bible. The first, the Abrahamic Covenant, is found in Genesis 12, 15, and 17. God chose Abraham and his descendants, later known as Israel, to be a nation for His own purposes and glory. The Abrahamic Covenant includes personal blessings for Abraham, national blessings for the Jewish people, and the universal blessing of the Messiah, Jesus, who would come through the line of Abraham and bring the gift of salvation to the world.

Next, we discussed the Mosaic Covenant and compared it with the New Covenant. We learned the Mosaic Covenant was conditional in nature, whereas the New Covenant is unconditional. While the blessings of the Mosaic Covenant were dependent upon *Israel's* faithfulness to God, the blessings of the New Covenant will be fulfilled because of *God's* faithfulness (2 Tim. 2:13). We also learned to recognize that when the New Testament uses the term "old covenant," it is referring to the Mosaic Covenant and not the entirety of the Hebrew Bible.

In this chapter, we will examine another major biblical covenant God established, this time with King David. The main texts for the Davidic Covenant are 2 Samuel 7 and 1 Chronicles 17. In these passages, we see God's love for Israel and the House of David, and His faithfulness to His covenant promises, which include the coming of a special Son of David to set up an eternal kingdom and reign forever.

THE PROMISES OF THE COVENANT

After many years of unrest, war, political intrigue, and living on the run, God had given David rest from his enemies on every side. With the kingdom at peace, David finally had time to think, pray, and consider things deep within his heart.

One idea returned to the king's mind and troubled him. How was it that he, a mere man, lived in a beautiful palace, while God was "residing" in a simple tent? His glory still dwelt in the tabernacle Moses had constructed in the wilderness. Surely the God of the universe deserved the finest palace in the world! This was the God who had redeemed his ancestors from Egypt and brought them to the promised land. This was the God who protected him when Saul had repeatedly sought to kill him. This was the God who led him to a decisive victory over the Jebusites, capturing their city—Jerusalem, from which he now reigned.

Perhaps God was offended that His ark was sheltered in a tent while David was surrounded by finery fit for a king. Perhaps that was David's task, to build a magnificent house for God.

David's thoughts were interrupted by a knock on the door. It was the prophet Nathan, David's friend. David proceeded to share what was on his mind, and Nathan was pleased by the king's desire to honor God. He encouraged David with these words, "Go and do all that is on your mind, for the Lord is with you."

However, as we read in 2 Samuel 7:4-17, God actually wakes Nathan up at night and gives him a message for David.

> But that night the word of the Lord came to Nathan: "Go to my servant David and say, 'This is what the Lord says: Are you to build me a house to dwell in? From the time I brought the Israelites out of Egypt until today I have not dwelt in a house; instead, I have been moving around

with a tent as my dwelling. In all my journeys with all the Israelites, have I ever spoken a word to one of the tribal leaders of Israel, whom I commanded to shepherd my people Israel, asking: Why haven't you built me a house of cedar?'

"So now this is what you are to say to my servant David: 'This is what the LORD of Armies says: I took you from the pasture, from tending the flock, to be ruler over my people Israel. I have been with you wherever you have gone, and I have destroyed all your enemies before you. I will make a great name for you like that of the greatest on the earth. I will designate a place for my people Israel and plant them, so that they may live there and not be disturbed again. Evildoers will not continue to oppress them as they have done ever since the day I ordered judges to be over my people Israel. I will give you rest from all your enemies.

"'The LORD declares to you: The LORD himself will make a house for you. When your time comes and you rest with your ancestors, I will raise up after you your descendant, who will come from your body, and I will establish his kingdom. He is the one who will build a house for my name, and I will establish the throne of his kingdom forever. I will be his father, and he will be my son. When he does wrong, I will discipline him with a rod of men and blows from mortals. But my faithful love will never leave him as it did when I removed it from Saul, whom I removed from before you. Your house and kingdom will endure before me forever, and your throne will be established forever.'"

Nathan reported all these words and this entire vision to David.

In addition to 2 Samuel 7, another complete account of the Davidic Covenant is located in 1 Chronicles 17:7-14. This covenant is also referenced in many other places throughout Scripture. Psalm 89, for example, expresses a hope for the fulfillment of the covenant God made with David. The New Testament also points to this covenant as a promise of the Messiah who would come from the line of David.[22]

The Biblical Background of the Covenant

Having some background information on the two biblical books where the Davidic Covenant is found in its entirety can give us helpful insight on the covenant itself. Today, our English Bibles have 1 and 2 Samuel as separate books, but in the Hebrew Bible, Samuel is actually just one book. Due to its length, the book was divided into two parts when the Hebrew Bible was first translated into Greek. This two-part division in our English Bibles doesn't compromise the reliability or divine inspiration of the Scriptures in any way, but we should keep in mind when reading 1 and 2 Samuel that they are in fact one cohesive whole.

Although the book bears Samuel's name, and the Talmud incorrectly attributes authorship to Samuel, he is likely not the author. The author is unknown. The book of Samuel alludes to the division of the kingdom in about 930 BC, but is completely silent on the fall of Israel to Assyria in 722 BC, which suggests that it was written sometime between these two major events (930–722 BC). The kingdom of Israel was divided during the reign of Rehoboam, Solomon's son, meaning the book of Samuel was written well after Solomon's rule. We will return to why this is important later.[23]

---

22   See Matthew 1:1; Luke 3:31; 2 Timothy 2:8; Revelation 22:16.
23   Winfred O. Neely, "1 Samuel," in *The Moody Bible Commentary*, eds. Michael Rydelnik and Michael Vanlaningham (Chicago: Moody Publishers, 2014), 399.

Like Samuel, 1 and 2 Chronicles are also just one book in the Hebrew Bible. The book of Chronicles is a record of Israelite history, with a focus on the House of David, and comes last in the order of books in the Hebrew canon. The Hebrew name for the book is דִּבְרֵי־הַיָּמִים (*Divrei-Hayamim*), which translates literally to "the words of the days." Based on the historical events detailed in Chronicles, the book can be dated to between 450–400 BC. This means Chronicles was penned possibly up to *five centuries* after the book of Samuel!

The Davidic Covenant has endured for the hundreds of years that elapsed between the writing of Samuel and Chronicles, and beyond. Its provisions and promises survived a divided kingdom, civil strife, idolatrous Baal worship, foreign wars, invasions, exiles, and the rise and fall of many kings. Despite all these tumultuous events, the hope of the Davidic Covenant remained among the Israelite faithful.

THE PROVISIONS OF THE COVENANT

Let's now look at the provisions of the Davidic Covenant. God begins by promising the people of Israel would be securely established in the land and live peacefully, with no enemies to oppress them (2 Sam. 7:10-11). Here, God is guaranteeing Israel permanent dwelling in the land and eternal rest, which was not fulfilled during the reign of David or Solomon. At a future time, Israel will enjoy these blessings forever under the reign of Jesus, the Son of David.

Instead of David building God a house to dwell in, God declares He will build a house—a dynasty—for David. This promise of a house anchors on a special descendant of David. "When your time comes and you rest with your ancestors," God says in verse 12, "I will raise up after you your descendant, who will come from your body, and I will establish his kingdom." God then gives David several specific promises concerning this descendant.

First in this series of promises is that God will establish the descendant's kingdom (v. 12). Second, God promises that the descendant would be the one to build Him a house, or a temple (v. 13). Third, in the latter part of verse 13, we read that the Davidic throne, which would one day belong to this descendant, would be established forever. Fourth, this descendant would have a relationship with God as a son does with his father (v. 14). Lastly, like the Abrahamic Covenant, God's covenant with David is *unconditional* and *eternal*. We see evidence for this in verses 15-16, where God assures that 1) His faithful love will never depart from David's descendant; and 2) David's house, kingdom, and throne will endure forever.

This leads us to an important question: who is the special descendant of David being referred to in this passage?

WHO WILL FULFILL THE COVENANT?

There are two primary views concerning the identity of the descendant in 2 Samuel 7 and 1 Chronicles 17. The first view holds that 2 Samuel is referring to Solomon, while 1 Chronicles pertains to a future Messiah. The second view suggests that the Messiah is being referred to in *both* passages, not Solomon. Interpreters on either side of the debate would agree that the Messiah is in view in 1 Chronicles, but they differ on who the descendant is in 2 Samuel. Below, we will make a case for the second view, that the descendant being referred to in both passages is the Messiah. We will also address two main objections to this interpretation.

Earlier on, we mentioned that the book of Samuel was most likely written between two major events in Israelite history: the division of the kingdom in 930 BC and the fall of the northern kingdom, Israel, to Assyria in 722 BC. Since this was after Solomon's time, the author of Samuel absolutely knew Solomon was not the son of David who would fulfill the covenant promises of 2 Samuel 7. The original readers of Samuel would have been familiar with Solomon's public failures, such as promiscuity and idolatry, so we can assume they also knew Solomon couldn't be the promised descendant. Therefore, it's unlikely that 2 Samuel 7 was intended to be a reference to Solomon.

Along with the chronological evidence, the interpretive guidance we find in the New Testament for 2 Samuel 7 also points us toward the second view. In Hebrews 1:5, the author quotes 2 Samuel 7:14 and 1 Chronicles 17:13, "I will be his Father, and he will be my Son," to demonstrate the Messiah's superiority to the angels. There is no doubt that the author of Hebrews, writing under the inspiration of the Holy Spirit, understood the promised descendant in the Davidic Covenant to be the Messiah. The attestation of the New Testament is a compelling reason for a messianic interpretation of 2 Samuel 7.

However, the same verse (2 Samuel 7:14) is also the source of one of the main objections to the Messiah being the intended referent. The second part of the verse reads, "When he does wrong, I will discipline him with a rod of men and blows from mortals." Some would argue that the text must be referring to a fallible human figure, because the Messiah would never do anything wrong.

This apparent conflict is resolved when we look at the text in Hebrew. The Hebrew word translated "when" in verse 14 is אֲשֶׁר (asher), but the same word can also be translated "if." In fact, when Jewish scholars were working on the Septuagint, a translation of the Hebrew Scriptures into Greek, they translated the word asher as "if," not "when." In other words, 2 Samuel 7:14 is not saying that the descendant of David will inevitably commit wrongdoing, but *if* he does, God will discipline him as a father disciplines his son. The original Hebrew text doesn't rule out the Messiah as the referent in this passage.

A second objection is derived from 2 Samuel 7:13, where God says of the special descendant, "He is the one who will build a house for my name, and I will establish the throne of his kingdom forever." Solomon was the one who built the first temple, so it seems to make sense that he would be the intended referent. Yet, even though Solomon oversaw the construction of a splendid temple for God, the throne of his kingdom wasn't established forever, and the temple was later destroyed. Zerubbabel built the second temple, but he never became king, let alone rule over an eternal kingdom. The Messiah is the one who will fulfill these covenant promises. For this reason, the prophets foretold that when He came, He would build a temple for the Lord (Zech. 6:13).

We know that the Messiah, Jesus, has already come. So where's the temple? Since the Romans destroyed the second temple in AD 70, there hasn't been a temple in Jerusalem. The promise of 2 Samuel 7:13 awaits a future fulfillment. When Jesus returns to set up the Millennial Kingdom, He will build a new temple and take His seat on the throne of David forever.[24]

CONCLUSION

Because of God's faithfulness to His promises, we can be sure there are Jewish people alive today who are members of the House of David, even if there is no human way to trace their lineage. Lineage is an important marker when it comes to recognizing the Messiah. In the Davidic Covenant, God provided a clue about the Messiah, that He would be a descendant of David. This is why Matthew begins his Gospel with an extensive

---

24   There are likely at least two more temples yet to be built in Jerusalem, beginning with the temple of the Tribulation Period. This temple will only last for a short time and will be defiled by the antichrist (Dan. 9:27; 2 Thess. 2:4). Next, when the Messiah comes to establish His kingdom, He will build a new, glorious temple. The descriptions of this future temple in the Millennial Kingdom are found in Ezekiel 40–48.

genealogy. The Messiah had to be Jewish, and he had to come from David's line. Matthew was demonstrating to his readers that Jesus' lineage fulfilled these messianic credentials.

As those who have put their faith in the Messiah, the Son of David, we can have confidence Jesus will one day build His temple and establish His reign over the whole world. In the meantime, we are to be "making the most of time" remaining (Eph. 5:16), in anticipation of Messiah's return for His bride, the church.

Listen to the episode for this chapter,
"An Overview of the Davidic Covenant,"
on The TŌV Podcast.

6

Restored and Regenerated

Ezekiel was a prophet-priest who ministered before and during the time of the Babylonian invasion. Hundreds of years prior to Ezekiel, in 722 BC, the northern kingdom of Israel had fallen to Assyria. In Ezekiel's day, the southern kingdom of Judah was facing the prospect of a similar exile, this time at the hands of Nebuchadnezzar. Judah faced this bleak outlook because they had persisted in the sin of idolatry and refused to heed the warnings of the prophets. As a consequence of their sin, God was using foreign nations as instruments of judgment to displace Judah from the land, just as He had done with the northern kingdom of Israel.

Ezekiel was exiled to Babylon at the same time as King Jehoiachin. Two more waves of deportations followed, culminating in 586 BC, when the Babylonian army exiled all who remained in Jerusalem, leaving only the poorest inhabitants behind. Led by Nebuzaradan, the captain of the guards, the army burned Solomon's temple to the ground, along with all the buildings in Jerusalem, and dismantled the walls surrounding the city. They left total devastation in their wake.

In the midst of these dire circumstances, the book of Ezekiel contains a resounding message of hope. Through the words of Ezekiel, God wanted Israel and the nations to know He had not forsaken His chosen people. He had plans to bring them back to the land for His name's sake. In this chapter, we will explore the promise of Israel's physical and spiritual restoration found in Ezekiel 36 and 37.

SETTING THE SCENE

In order to understand Ezekiel 36, we need to turn back to chapter 35, where Ezekiel is commanded by God to prophesy against Mount Seir. Here, Mount Seir represents the nation of Edom.

> Because you maintained a perpetual hatred and gave the Israelites over to the power of the sword in the time of their disaster, the time of final punishment, therefore, as I live—this is the declaration of the Lord GOD—I will destine you for bloodshed, and it will pursue you. Since you did not hate bloodshed, it will pursue you. (vv. 5-6)

The anger and jealousy Edom harbored toward Israel has not gone unnoticed by God. In fact, by speaking blasphemously and arrogantly against the mountains of Israel, Edom has spoken against God Himself (vv. 12-13). God will not let Edom go unpunished for this transgression. Because they rejoiced at Israel's destruction, God would make Edom a desolate wasteland.

In Ezekiel 36, mountains are again used as a representation for an entire nation, but now God turns from pronouncing judgment on Edom to blessing Israel. He calls Ezekiel to prophesy to the mountains of Israel, as well as to the "hills, to the ravines and valleys, to the desolate ruins and abandoned cities, which have become plunder and a mockery to the rest of the nations all around" (v. 4). God has "burning zeal" for the people and the land of Israel, which are His possession, and He will not allow the nations who gleefully claimed the land and ravaged it to go unpunished (v. 5).

THE ONE WHO CURSES YOU I WILL CURSE

When God established His covenant with Abraham in Genesis, one of the covenant promises was that He would bless those who bless Abraham and His descendants, and "curse anyone who treats you with contempt" (Gen. 12:3a). In Ezekiel 36, we see God providing assurance of His faithfulness to the Abrahamic Covenant. The nations Ezekiel prophesied against will pay a high price for trampling God's chosen nation under their feet.

Because Israel has endured the insults of the nations, God swears that "the nations all around you will endure their own insults" (Ezek. 36:7). Even today, it's hard to find another nation that has been condemned, slandered, or vilified more than Israel.

Take the United Nations as just one example. In 1975, the UN voted to condemn Zionism (the view that the Jewish state should exist and be able to defend itself) as a form of racism. According to the UN, if someone believed the most persecuted group of people on earth should be able to defend themselves in their own homeland, they were a racist. This UN resolution was reversed in 1991,[25] but the damage to Israel's reputation had already been done. Unfortunately, the word and concept of "Zionism" is now perceived by many, including some Christians, as something negative.

In addition, the UN Human Rights Council (UNHCR) lists Israel as a standing agenda item. According to unwatch.org, a Geneva-based NGO who monitors the performance of the United Nations, Israel has been condemned by the UN General Assembly a total of 115 times since 2015. In striking contrast, the countries of Iran, North Korea, Syria, and China have been

---

25   John M. Goshko, "U.N. Repeals Resolution Linking Zionism to Racism," *The Washington Post*, December 17, 1991, https://www.washingtonpost.com/archive/politics/1991/12/17/un-repeals-resolution-linking-zionism-to-racism/70349a7c-ae07-40ea-b37d-ee711e0636eb/.

condemned a total of 28 times *combined*.[26] As Danny Danon, Israel's former ambassador to the UN, said, "At the UN, if you stay neutral, you are against Israel."[27]

ISRAEL'S TWOFOLD RESTORATION: PHYSICAL AND SPIRITUAL

As Ezekiel 36 unfolds, God declares in verses 8-12 that He will make the land of Israel fruitful and inhabited:

> You, mountains of Israel, will produce your branches and bear your fruit for my people Israel, since their arrival is near. Look! I am on your side; I will turn toward you, and you will be tilled and sown. I will fill you with people, with the whole house of Israel in its entirety. The cities will be inhabited and the ruins rebuilt. I will fill you with people and animals, and they will increase and be fruitful. I will make you inhabited as you once were and make you better off than you were before. Then you will know that I am the LORD. I will cause people, my people Israel, to walk on you; they will possess you, and you will be their inheritance. You will no longer deprive them of their children.

Some of Israel's enemies had been saying of the mountains of Israel, "You devour people and deprive your nation of children" (v. 13). God would remove any grounds for this insult by transforming Israel into a land overflowing with life and abundance. There is no reason these descriptions should not be taken to mean that Israel will literally experience physical regeneration when the Messiah is ruling over a restored Israel in the Millennial Kingdom.

---

26   "UN Watch Database," UN Watch, n.d., https://unwatch.org/database/.

27   Danny Danon, *In the Lion's Den: Israel and the World* (Wicked Son, 2022), 95, Kindle.

Beginning in verse 16, Ezekiel reminds his audience what had led them to be scattered among the nations. Because of Israel's sinful conduct and actions, which included idolatry, the land had been defiled. God responded by pouring out His judgment in the form of exile, but the Gentile nations saw the displacement of the Jewish people as a sign of God's failure to keep His people in the land He had given them. God's name had been dishonored among the Gentiles who witnessed the disgrace of Israel's exile.

We read God's response in verse 21: "Then I had concern for my holy name, which the house of Israel profaned among the nations where they went." Often, when we study the prophets and read about what God will do for Israel and the Jewish people in the future, we get the wrong message that God's actions are dependent *on Israel's good behavior*. However, the Bible repeatedly teaches that God acts not for the sake of Israel, but *for His holy name* (v. 22). Israel represents God to the nations, and God cares about His reputation.[28]

In the next portion of Ezekiel 36, we learn the restoration of Israel will not only be physical but also spiritual:

> For I will take you from the nations and gather you from all the countries, and will bring you into your own land. I will also sprinkle clean water on you, and you will be clean. I will cleanse you from all your impurities and all your idols. I will give you a new heart and put a new spirit within you; I will remove your heart of stone and give you a heart of flesh. *I will place my Spirit within you and cause you to follow my statutes and carefully observe my ordinances.* You will live in the land that I gave your ancestors; *you will be my people, and I will be your God.* I will save you from all your uncleanness. (vv. 24-29a, emphasis added)

28 See Ezekiel 20:9, 14, 22, 44.

Earlier, in verse 17, God likened Israel's sin to menstrual impurity, an allusion to Leviticus 15. Under the Mosaic Law, sprinkling or washing with water was done to purify someone from ceremonial uncleanliness. In the context of this passage from Ezekiel, God's act of sprinkling clean water on Israel signifies cleansing from sin, which will be followed by the giving of new life. Israel will receive a new heart that is no longer hardened toward God and be indwelled by the Holy Spirit. If this sounds familiar, it's because Ezekiel is making a reference to the New Covenant, which we looked at in chapter 4.

In Jeremiah 31, where the terms of the New Covenant are most explicitly recorded, God declares, "'Instead, this is the covenant I will make with the house of Israel after those days'—the LORD's declaration. 'I will put my teaching within them and write it on their hearts. I will be their God, and they will be my people'" (v. 33).

Those partaking of the New Covenant blessings will be inwardly transformed by God's Spirit. When God redeems Israel and gives them a new heart, they will be able to fully enjoy the blessings of being a nation set apart for His purposes. Those who recognize that God's future redemption of Israel is about His name, glory and purposes—not about the merits or behavior of the Jewish people—are often excited for God's work among His chosen nation. They are often prayer warriors for the Jewish people. But those who only see the Jewish people as just another people group (or worse) are often blinded to what God is doing and what He will do as He uses Israel to broadcast His great name among the nations. This is why the prophet Jeremiah urges the nations to proclaim God's promises and dealings with Israel among the Gentiles.[29]

One of the blessings of the New Covenant, as we read in Ezekiel 36:29b-30, is the absence of famine in the land. Instead of

29   See Jeremiah 31:10-11.

scarcity, food will abound. When Israel receives this outpouring of God's grace and goodness, the nation will realize the sinfulness of their former ways and experience genuine remorse for what they had done (vv. 31-32). The fruitfulness of the land will make it comparable to the garden of Eden (v. 35). Cities will be rebuilt and reinhabited, and God will multiply the population of Israel like the flocks of sheep gathered in Jerusalem during major holidays (vv. 35, 37-38). God's restoration of Israel will be a testimony of who He is, for Israel and the nations (vv. 36, 38).

THE TIMING OF ISRAEL'S RESTORATION

At this point, you may be wondering when these dramatic events take place. Some interpreters would say the prophecy in Ezekiel 36 was fulfilled when Israel returned from Babylon during the ministries of Ezra and Nehemiah. But if we read the text carefully, we'll see the scope of Israel's restoration, as described in Ezekiel 36 and so many other prophetic passages, far exceeds what Israel experienced when they returned to the land from Babylonian exile.

Ezekiel 36 describes an Israel that is flourishing both physically and spiritually. We have not yet witnessed such a phenomenon. The post-exilic nation of Israel, beginning with Ezra's recorded return, does not even come close to fitting this description. Today, although the process of physical restoration to their ancient homeland has begun, more Jewish people live outside Israel than in the land.[30] Moreover, the vast majority of Jewish people haven't yet placed their faith in Jesus as their Messiah. Therefore, it's more fitting to see Ezekiel's prophecy as pointing

---

30   More than half the world's 15.7 million Jewish population are in the diaspora; 7.2 million (46%) live in Israel. TOI Staff, "Global Jewish population hits 15.7 million ahead of new year, 46% of them in Israel," *The Times of Israel*, September 15, 2023, https://www.timesofisrael.com/global-jewish-population-hits-15-7-million-ahead-of-new-year-46-of-them-in-israel/.

to a *yet future* restoration of Israel, which will take place after the Messiah returns and establishes His kingdom on earth.

THE TWO STAGES OF ISRAEL'S RESTORATION

Since the full restoration of Israel is a yet future event, how do we make sense of the modern nation of Israel, which has served as a home and refuge for millions of Jewish people since its founding in 1948? Does the Bible say anything about modern Israel, or explain why Jewish people are returning to the land but remaining in unbelief? God's revelation to Ezekiel in chapter 37 can help guide us in understanding where the modern state of Israel fits in God's plan of redemption.

"The hand of the LORD was on me," Ezekiel recounts at the beginning of chapter 37, "and he brought me out by his Spirit and set me down in the middle of the valley; it was full of bones." The bones blanketing this valley had been there long enough that the sun had dried them out. God asked Ezekiel, "Son of man, can these bones live?" to which Ezekiel replied, "Lord GOD, only you know" (v. 3). Ezekiel humbly acknowledged that God alone has the power to bring the dead to life.

God commanded Ezekiel to prophesy to these dry bones, saying, "I will cause breath to enter you, and you will live. I will put tendons on you, make flesh grow on you, and cover you with skin. I will put breath in you so that you come to life. Then you will know that I am the LORD" (vv. 5-6).

Ezekiel obeyed, and as he spoke, the air began to quiver with the sound of rattling. Imagine the miracle unfolding before Ezekiel's eyes: millions of bones assembling themselves into whole skeletons, connected by joints, knit together by tendons, and finally covered in flesh and skin. But the bodies were lifeless— "there was no breath in them" (v. 8). God instructed Ezekiel to prophesy a second time:

> He said to me, "Prophesy to the breath, prophesy, son
> of man. Say to it: This is what the Lord GOD says: Breath,
> come from the four winds and breathe into these slain so
> that they may live!" So I prophesied as he commanded
> me; the breath entered them, and they came to life and
> stood on their feet, a vast army. (vv. 9-10)

God then identified the bones as "the whole house of Israel" (v. 11). Notice how the restoration of Israel in this vision—from bones scattered over a parched valley to living people forming the ranks of an army—happened in two stages. First, God declares in verse 12, "I am going to open your graves and bring you up from them, my people, and lead you into the land of Israel." During the first stage, God will regather the Jewish people to the land, but they will be spiritually lifeless, just as the bodies in Ezekiel's vision were without breath.

Then, after Israel is physically restored to the land, the second stage is spiritual revival. As God says in verses 13-14, "You will know that I am the LORD, my people, when I open your graves and bring you up from them. I will put my Spirit in you, and you will live, and I will settle you in your own land. Then you will know that I am the LORD. I have spoken, and I will do it. This is the declaration of the LORD." The Hebrew word for breath, רוּחַ (*ruah*), which appears many times in Ezekiel 37, can also be translated "wind" or "spirit." The breath that revives the dry bones is symbolic of the Holy Spirit's work in resurrecting the nation of Israel by bringing them into a saving relationship with the Jewish Messiah, Jesus.

I believe we are witnessing the fulfillment of the first stage of Ezekiel's dry bones vision. God, in His divine sovereignty, is calling Jewish people back to the land. This is why the spiritual opposition to Israel's existence is so fierce. Satan knows that God has made promises to preserve the Jewish people, return them to their homeland, and regenerate them spiritually. Just as believers experience spiritual opposition when we engage in God's work, so Satan opposes God's plans for Israel every step of the way. Ultimately, Satan is the instigator of all attempts to destroy God's people. It is a satanic spirit, marked by antisemitism, that was behind Nazi ideology. It is a satanic spirit behind the murderous actions and ideology of Hamas, Hezbollah, and the Houthis. And it is a satanic spirit behind the mullahs of Iran, who publicly declare their desire to wipe Israel off the map. These enemies of Israel, for whom we should pray, are blinded by Satan and unknowingly doing his bidding. Unfortunately, they are paying, and will continue to pay, a very high price (Gen. 12:3).

In God's sovereign timing, the second stage of Ezekiel's prophecy will take place in the end times. Then, Israel will recognize Jesus as their Messiah and cry out for His return. The prophet Zechariah describes this same national repentance in Zechariah 12:10, writing, "Then I will pour out a spirit of grace and prayer on the house of David and the residents of Jerusalem, and they will look at me whom they pierced. They will mourn for him as one mourns for an only child and weep bitterly for him as one weeps for a firstborn."

Jesus also spoke of the circumstances of His second coming as He wept over Jerusalem in Luke 13:34-35:

> Jerusalem, Jerusalem, who kills the prophets and stones those who are sent to her. How often I wanted to gather your children together, as a hen gathers her chicks under her wings, but you were not willing! See, your house is abandoned to you. I tell you, you will not see me until the time comes when you say, "Blessed is he who comes in the name of the Lord!"

In Hebrew, "Blessed is he who comes in the name of the Lord" is *"Baruch haba b'shem Adonai."* The next time Israel sees Jesus, they will welcome Him because they recognize Him as their Messiah. The second coming will be an earth-shattering event (literally), with the Messiah descending on the Mount of Olives to fight against the nations invading Jerusalem and to provide miraculous deliverance for the city's inhabitants (see Zechariah 14).

THE FUTURE REUNIFICATION OF ISRAEL

Ezekiel 37 closes with another stunning prophecy that the prophet delivers to his audience through an object lesson. God instructed Ezekiel to take two sticks and label one stick with the name Judah, representing Israel's southern kingdom, and the other stick with Joseph or Ephraim, representing the northern kingdom. Ezekiel was to join these two sticks together "into a single stick so that they become one in your hand" (v. 17), and he was to explain to those who inquired about the meaning of his object lesson that God intended to unify the divided kingdoms of Israel.

The separation of Israel into a northern and southern kingdom occurred shortly after Solomon's reign. Not only had the kingdom been divided for centuries, but the northern kingdom had fallen to Assyria in 722 BC, and the southern kingdom was taken in recurring waves into exile by Babylon from 605–586 BC. Ezekiel was among those deported to Babylon, and he could not have ministered during a more precarious time in Israel's history.

In the midst of Israel's devastation, God gave Ezekiel a message of hope for the exiles. One day, God would gather the Jewish people as "one nation in the land, on the mountains of Israel, and one king will rule over all of them" (v. 22). This king is called "my servant David" and "shepherd" in verse 24. At the time of Ezekiel's writing, long after King David's death, his name had already become synonymous with the Messiah in prophetic literature. Ezekiel was teaching that the Messiah would reign over a restored Israel.

CONCLUSION

When Jesus returns and sets up the Millennial Kingdom, a unified Israel will be empowered by the Spirit to walk in obedience to God (v. 24). They will live permanently in the land God gave to Abraham, Isaac, and Jacob. Under the eternal reign of the Prince of Peace (v. 25), God will establish a peace covenant with Israel and "set [His] sanctuary among them forever" (v. 26). This future sanctuary will be a physical temple, whose measurements, worship, and other features are delineated in Ezekiel 40–48. With Israel dwelling in the land and reconciled to God, and God's temple established in their midst forever, the nations will know that God is the one who sanctifies Israel (v. 28).

Listen to The TŌV Podcast episodes for this chapter:

"Israel's Future: Ezekiel 36 Explained"

"Ezekiel 37 Explained"

7

The Future Battle for Jerusalem

No city in the world plays a more prominent role in the Bible than the city of Jerusalem. Despite its Hebrew name, *Yerushalayim*, meaning "City of Peace," Jerusalem has often experienced the exact opposite. Massacres, terrorism, and catastrophic wars have left indelible scars on the city and its inhabitants. Sadly, according to the Hebrew prophets, Jerusalem will continue to be a locus of violent conflict in the future. In this chapter, we will take an in-depth look at Zechariah 14 to learn about a major battle that will take place in and around Jerusalem at the close of the Tribulation Period.

The book of Zechariah was written by the Hebrew prophet Zechariah in the early fifth century BC.[31] Prior to the book's completion, Cyrus the Great had issued his decree that permitted Jewish people to return to the land, effectively ending the Babylonian exile. Not all the exiles chose to make the journey back, but those who did so faced discouragement and hardship. Solomon's temple remained in ruins, and there were no walls to provide security or defense for the city of Jerusalem. Poverty, a lack of rain, and land that failed to yield produce in spite of the people's labors made life in Judah exceedingly difficult. This was a far cry from the glory days of David and Solomon!

---

31   Michael Rydelnik, "Zechariah," in *The Moody Bible Commentary*, eds. Michael Rydelnik and Michael Vanlaningham (Chicago: Moody Publishers, 2014), 1414.

Zechariah had an important message for the inhabitants of Jerusalem who had survived the exile. Their circumstances were distressing, their future was uncertain, and they knew their disobedience to God had prompted Him to remove them from the land for a time. Yet, as 2 Timothy 2:13 tells us, "If we are faithless, he [God] remains faithful, for he cannot deny himself." Part of Zechariah's message involved revealing God's plan to personally rescue Jerusalem during a future time of abject suffering.

THE END-TIMES SIEGE OF JERUSALEM

You're probably familiar with the question, "Do you want the good news first, or the bad news?" In Zechariah 14, Zechariah chooses to start off with the bad news. He writes,

> Look, a day belonging to the LORD is coming when the plunder taken from you will be divided in your presence. I will gather all the nations against Jerusalem for battle. The city will be captured, the houses looted, and the women raped. Half the city will go into exile, but the rest of the people will not be removed from the city. (vv. 1-2)

Zechariah paints a bleak picture of the future of Jerusalem, where the city will again be torn apart by violence and exile. This scene will take place at the end of the seven-year Tribulation, when the antichrist will deceive and wield power over the whole world (Rev. 13:5, 7). The second half of the Tribulation will be a time of unprecedented persecution for the Jewish people, culminating in the battle described by Zechariah, when Jerusalem is besieged by the nations and the people of the city are trapped.

Under the leadership of the antichrist, the armies of the nations will gather in the Jezreel Valley, where the ruins of the famous ancient city Megiddo are still visible today. If we combine the Hebrew word for mountain (*har*) and Meggido, we get Har Megiddo (literally the "Mountain of Megiddo"), which appears in most English Bibles as Armageddon (Rev. 16:16). It is from this ancient location, Megiddo, that this apocalyptic battle gets its name.

At this critical moment in the battle, God Himself will descend and fight against Jerusalem's enemies (Zech. 14:3). In other words, the one who comes to deliver Israel is none other than the Lord Jesus! Verse 4 tells us, "On that day his feet will stand on the Mount of Olives, which faces Jerusalem on the east. The Mount of Olives will be split in half from east to west, forming a huge valley, so that half the mountain will move to the north and half to the south."

Zechariah's prophecy corresponds with what the disciples were told by two angels as they watched the resurrected Jesus being taken up into heaven: "Men of Galilee, why do you stand looking up into heaven? This same Jesus, who has been taken from you into heaven, will come in the same way that you have seen him going into heaven" (Acts 1:11).

It's no accident that Jesus' ascension took place on the Mount of Olives (v. 12). At the end of the Tribulation, Jesus will return in His physical, glorified body, touch down on the same mountain, and create an escape route for those in Jerusalem by *splitting the entire mountain in half!*

The people in the besieged city will flee through this newly created valley, "for the valley of the mountains will extend to Azal," just as they fled from the earthquake in the days of King Uzziah of Judah (Zech. 14:5). Then the Lord Jesus will enter into battle with His holy ones. These holy ones are likely believers who were previously raptured, and are seen returning with the Lord. Zechariah tells us this will be "a unique day known only to the LORD," with the absence of light until the evening making day and night indistinguishable from each other (vv. 6-7). He then describes several topographical changes that will occur "on that day" when Jesus becomes "King over the whole earth" (v. 9).

Notice how Zechariah prophesies that Jesus will set up His kingdom *on the earth.* The Millennial Kingdom is a real, physical kingdom that will be established on earth for a thousand years. When we die as believers, our spirits go immediately to be with God, but at the resurrection we will be given restored, supernatural bodies, just as Jesus was given a new body after He was raised. We will inhabit the earth physically, both during the Millennial Kingdom and eternally afterward, when there will be a new heaven, a new earth, and a new Jerusalem (Rev. 21:1–2). We will examine this period more closely in the next chapter. For now, let's return to Zechariah's topographical changes that will take place after the Messiah's return.

JERUSALEM'S SURROUNDINGS TRANSFORMED

In Zechariah 14:8, we read "living water will flow out from Jerusalem, half of it toward the eastern sea [the Dead Sea] and the other half toward the western sea [the Mediterranean], in summer and winter alike." This river is the same one Ezekiel saw in a vision "flowing from under the threshold of the temple toward the east" (Ezek. 47:1).

Not only will there be a river with a supernatural source flowing from the temple, but "all the land from Geba to Rimmon south of Jerusalem will be changed into a plain" (Zech. 14:10a). At present, the land surrounding Jerusalem is marked by foothills and valleys, causing spikes and plunges in elevation. In the future, this uneven terrain will be transformed into a plain, and the city of Jerusalem will stand out above it.

Zechariah writes that "Jerusalem will be raised up and will remain on its site from the Benjamin Gate to the place of the First Gate, to the Corner Gate, and from the Tower of Hananel to the royal winepresses" (v. 10b). While we don't know where all these landmarks are in Jerusalem today, they clearly existed in Zechariah's day, and he was making a point that the location of the city would remain the same despite the nations' attempts to obliterate it. The inhabitants of Jerusalem will finally experience perfect peace under Jesus, the Prince of Peace. "People will live there, and never again will there be a curse of complete destruction. So Jerusalem will dwell in security" (v. 11).

THE PUNISHMENT OF JERUSALEM'S INVADERS

The nations who arrayed themselves against Jerusalem at the battle of Armageddon will not go unpunished. God will strike them with a terrible plague that causes their flesh, their eyes, and their tongues to rot. Not only that, but God will also cause "a great panic" to seize the invaders so they will turn on one another in confusion (v. 13). It seems God will empower Judah to join the battle and to plunder their attackers, seizing an abundance of gold, silver, and clothing (v. 14). Meanwhile, all the animals in the camps of the nations—horses, mules, camels, and donkeys—will be struck with the same rotting plague God had inflicted on their human masters (v. 15).

But will there actually be animals at the battle of Armageddon? Many interpreters argue these descriptions shouldn't be taken literally. Some speculate the biblical authors may have witnessed modern military equipment, but because they didn't understand what they were seeing, they opted to describe the unfamiliar technology as animals.

The difficulty with this explanation is that most of us can tell the difference between an animal and something man-made, even if we've never been exposed to it before. It seems unlikely that Zechariah would choose to describe military technology as animals when they had manufactured devices from their own time (such as boats and chariots) that might have been more naturally evoked by what they saw.

We may wonder if Zechariah is using animals symbolically in verse 15, but a symbolic interpretation isn't necessary to make sense of the verse. Today, we live in an increasingly interconnected world, and we've experienced how rapidly the world can change in times of crisis. It's possible that an unexpected turn of events in the future will force armies to revert to ancient forms of transportation—whether it be a fuel shortage, or something else that prevents the use of advanced military equipment. It's also possible animals will be used alongside modern military equipment, and Zechariah just did not include those details.

THE MESSIAH WILL REIGN FROM JERUSALEM

When we come to Zechariah 14:16, the scene shifts to what life will be like for the nations in the Millennial Kingdom. We read in verse 16, "Then all the survivors from the nations that came against Jerusalem will go up year after year to worship the King, the LORD of Armies, and to celebrate the Festival of Shelters." There will be those among the nations who put their faith in Jesus during the Tribulation Period. In the Millennial Kingdom, when Jesus reigns from Jerusalem, these survivors will make an annual trip there to worship Him and take part in the Festival of Shelters, also known as the Feast of Tabernacles/Booths, or Sukkot.

Sukkot is named for the *sukkah* ("booth," singular) the Israelites traditionally built for the festival, to celebrate God tabernacling with His people. This holiday remains widely celebrated in the Jewish community, and it will be an especially fitting festival for all nations in the millennium when Jesus, the divine King, will dwell on earth with His subjects.

Zechariah informs us the nations are free to choose whether they will obey the King in going up to Jerusalem to worship and celebrate, but God will punish those who refuse by withholding rain from their land. Egypt is specifically named in this passage, implying that distinct nations will exist in God's future kingdom (vv. 17-19).

In the Millennial Kingdom, the fear and knowledge of God will be so widespread that a strict divide between the sacred and profane will no longer be needed. Even the most ordinary items like horses' bells and cooking pots will be consecrated for use in worship (v. 20). "Every pot in Jerusalem and in Judah will be holy to the LORD of Armies," Zechariah writes. "All who sacrifice will come and use the pots to cook in. And on that day there will no longer be a Canaanite in the house of the LORD of Armies" (v. 21). (A Canaanite in this context refers to an unclean person.)

Let's return for a moment to the sacrifices mentioned in verse 21. It may come as a surprise that there will be sacrifices in the Millennial Kingdom. Our immediate reaction might be something like, "I thought we were done with sacrifices, since the Messiah's sacrifice was once for all." This is true with respect to the sacrifice for the atonement of sins. Jesus' death and resurrection accomplished what the blood of bulls and goats could never do, and for those who respond to His sacrifice with belief, their sins are completely removed.

The Bible doesn't tell us *why* there will continue to be sacrifices in the Millennial Kingdom, but the best guess we have is that these future sacrifices are for memorial purposes. They will not be efficacious for removing sins; they instead point back to the ultimate, all-sufficient sacrifice of Jesus. In this way, such sacrifices serve as reminders similar to what we presently experience when we partake of the Lord's Supper.

CONCLUSION

In the next and final chapter, we will examine this future time referred to as the Millennial Kingdom. For centuries, many in the church have been unaware of the prophecies concerning this kingdom. Is it going to be a literal, earthly kingdom or a spiritual one? Where does this kingdom fit on the eschatological timeline? And who will be present in this kingdom? We seek to address those questions and more in the following pages!

Listen to the episode for this chapter, "The Future Battle for Jerusalem," on The TŌV Podcast.

8

Demystifying the Millennial Kingdom

WHY STUDY THE MILLENNIAL KINGDOM?

The Millennial Kingdom gets its name from the millennium John writes about in Revelation 20, where it's revealed that the duration of Jesus' reign will be one thousand years. Yet, even though we find this prophecy about the Messiah's future reign in the last book of the Bible, we'd be mistaken to think the doctrine of the Millennial Kingdom was added as an afterthought. In fact, as theologian Michael Vlach maintains,

> The millennium is not some incidental doctrine that doesn't really matter. It is a major part of the Bible's storyline and involves the nature and timing of Jesus' kingdom. The idea of a future earthly kingdom of the Messiah is not something dropped from the sky in Revelation 20. It has deep roots back to Genesis 1.[32]

One reason we should study the Millennial Kingdom is because it is an integral part of the scriptural narrative. It is a common thread running through the majority of the prophetic books. Arnold Fruchtenbaum makes the observation that "every writing prophet, with the exception of just four: Jonah, Nahum, Habakkuk, and Malachi, had something to say about the Millennial Kingdom."[33] In other words, if we leave the Millennial

---

32   Michael Vlach, *Premillennialism: Why There Must Be a Future Earthly Kingdom of Jesus* (Theological Studies Press, 2017), 7.
33   Arnold Fruchtenbaum, *The Footsteps of the Messiah: A Study of the Sequence of Prophetic Events* (Ariel Ministries, 2004), 403.

Kingdom out of our studies of the Bible, we are missing a vital component of the Bible's teaching!

In addition to the prophets, it appears the Millennial Kingdom was also a significant point of interest for Jesus' disciples. In Acts 1:6-7, the disciples were with the resurrected Messiah, and they asked him, "Lord, are you restoring the kingdom to Israel at this time?" The disciples were familiar with what the Hebrew prophets wrote concerning the future of Israel, and they were expecting the Messiah to bring in His kingdom.

Notice how Jesus responded. He didn't rebuke the disciples for asking the question, or tell them that the plans have changed and He was going to usher in a spiritual kingdom instead of a literal, material one. Jesus simply said, "It is not for you to know times or periods that the Father has set by his own authority." The disciples didn't need to know the time of the kingdom's arrival, but they could count on the fact that the Messiah *would* establish His kingdom sometime in the future.

THREE VIEWS ON THE MILLENNIAL KINGDOM

Now that we've covered some reasons to study the Millennial Kingdom, let's look at the three most popular views concerning Jesus' thousand-year reign: the premillennial, amillennial, and postmillennial views.

The premillennial view proposes that Jesus will return *before* ("pre") the establishment of the Millennial Kingdom, and that the kingdom itself will be future, literal, and located on earth.

By contrast, the amillennial view holds that there is *no* future Millennial Kingdom (the prefix "a" in "amillennial" means none or without). From the amillennial perspective, passages in the Bible about the Millennial Kingdom are being fulfilled spiritually right now in the church age. At this moment, Jesus is reigning in the hearts of believers. Since we are already living in the kingdom, according to the amillennial view, there is no need to look forward to a literal, thousand-year reign of Jesus on earth.

Postmillennialists believe the return of Jesus will happen *after* ("post") the millennium, which they understand figuratively to mean a considerable period of time, not literally one thousand years. Those who adhere to this position interpret Jesus' parables comparing the kingdom to a mustard seed that grows into a tree, or to leaven that is worked through a lump of dough, as indicating Jesus will come again when the nations are evangelized and the majority of people on earth are His followers (Matt. 13:31-33). The postmillennial view projects that the world will progressively get better and better until the second coming of Messiah.

In the next section, we will look at several passages from Scripture and make a case for the premillennial understanding of the future kingdom of Messiah.

EVIDENCE FOR THE PREMILLENNIAL VIEW

Revelation 5:10

In Revelation 5, John the apostle was experiencing a vision of God's throne room in heaven. He saw a scroll with seven seals, but wept because nobody was found worthy to open it—until Jesus appeared on the scene as the Lamb of God. He alone is worthy! As He took the scroll and prepared to open its seals, the throne room resounded with a new song of praise, which included these lines:

> You made them a kingdom
> and priests to our God,
> and they will reign on the earth. (v. 10)

From these inspired lyrics, we learn there will be a future kingdom in which believers from every tribe, language, people and nation will be reigning together with the Lord Jesus. Moreover, the location of their reign will be on the earth.

1 Corinthians 4:7-8

Paul's first letter to the Corinthian church addresses many areas where the believers in Corinth had strayed from the gospel in their beliefs and conduct. In 1 Corinthians 4, Paul confronts the Corinthians about their pride, writing,

> For who makes you so superior? What do you have that you didn't receive? If, in fact, you did receive it, why do you boast as if you hadn't received it? You are already full! You are already rich! You have begun to reign as kings without us—and I wish you did reign, so that we could also reign with you! (vv. 7-8)

In these verses, Paul is trying (with a heavy dose of sarcasm) to correct the Corinthians' superior attitude. The Corinthian believers mistakenly thought they were already reigning as kings, when in reality Jesus' splendid kingdom and their co-reigning with Him was yet to come. The future arrival of this kingdom remains something we as believers should anticipate today.[34]

Matthew 19:28

When Peter asked Jesus what reward there will be for those who have left everything behind to follow Him, Jesus replied, "Truly I tell you, in the renewal of all things, when the Son of Man sits on his glorious throne, you who have followed me will also sit on twelve thrones, judging the twelve tribes of Israel."

Here, Jesus is teaching about the future Messianic Age, another term for the Millennial Kingdom. We learn from this verse that

---

34   Vlach, *Premillennialism*, 48.

the Son of Man will rule this kingdom from His glorious throne. His disciples will also have positions of authority, and they will govern the twelve tribes of Israel. Jesus' answer to Peter indicates that the Millennial Kingdom will be a literal (not spiritual) domain, one in which Israel will exist as a distinct nation.

Jeremiah 31:31-34

In this passage, Jeremiah prophesies that God will establish a New Covenant with the people of Israel, one that will be superior to the Mosaic Covenant. This New Covenant includes the promise of the full spiritual restoration of the whole nation of Israel. This is why Paul could write in Romans 11:26 that "all Israel will be saved." Not only was he writing under the inspiration of the Spirit, but Paul would have encountered this promise as he read the prophetic books, including Jeremiah.

When Jesus returns and sets up His Messianic Kingdom, the people of Israel will finally be spiritually restored to God and physically restored to the land given to Abraham and his descendants. God's specific plan for Israel in the Millennial Kingdom is further evidence that this kingdom will be a literal, future, earthly reality.

WHERE DOES THE MILLENNIAL KINGDOM FIT ON THE TIMELINE?

We now come to the question, *When* does Jesus begin His earthly reign? In this section, we will look at a few passages from the Bible that provide reference points for when the Millennial Kingdom will be established.

First, in Matthew 25:31, as Jesus was telling parables about the kingdom of heaven, He said, "When the Son of Man comes in his glory, and all the angels with him, then he will sit on his glorious throne." This short verse tells us that at Jesus' second coming, He will return in terrifying power with a great host of angels, and *then* He will take His throne. The Messianic Kingdom comes after the Lord's return to earth.

If you recall from previous chapters, Jesus will return when Israel recognizes Him as the Messiah and cries out for deliverance from the nations besieging Jerusalem (see Zech. 12:10; 14). John records in Revelation 19 how the Messiah will utterly destroy the invading armies in His fierce anger. Then, in Revelation 20, we are told Jesus will reign with His saints for one thousand years. We see in these two chapters a sequence of events in which the Millennial Kingdom is set up by Jesus *after* His second coming and victory.

Want to learn more? Listen to this TŌV Podcast episode on the sequence of end-times events.

You may be wondering, *Since Jesus is God, doesn't He already have the right to reign right now?* Absolutely! Indeed, God is currently ruling over all creation, and He is sovereign over everything. But we have to be careful not to confuse God's present, universal reign with the Messiah's reign in the Millennial Kingdom. Unlike God's universal reign, which is eternal and unlimited by space, the Messianic Kingdom will be located on earth, and it will have a beginning and an end.

One final note about the timing of the Millennial Kingdom: it is a time of worldwide peace. As Isaiah writes concerning the Messianic Age in Isaiah 2:4,

> [God] will settle disputes among the nations
> and provide arbitration for many peoples.
> They will beat their swords into plows
> and their spears into pruning knives.

Nation will not take up the sword against nation,
and they will never again train for war.

People living during this time will seek God's righteous instruction to obey it. God will serve as a fair and perfect judge over the earth, and there will no longer be cause for violent dispute. Weapons will be refashioned into agricultural tools. Wars will be a thing of the past.

Clearly, we are not living in an age that fits this description. None of us would look back on the last hundred years of human history as a time of peace, and there continue to be terrible wars, diseases, terrorism, poverty, and starvation all over the globe. Israel remains surrounded by hostile nations and repeatedly is traumatized by horrific terrorist attacks. The existence of so much suffering and conflict today precludes the possibility that we are already in the Millennial Kingdom (the amillennial view) or that things are steadily improving as the second coming of Messiah draws near (the postmillennial view). We're not there yet, but the day is coming.

When Jesus returns and sets up the Messianic Kingdom, He will inaugurate a much better age than the one we currently live in. But even when the Prince of Peace rules in righteousness, things will not be perfect. There will nonetheless be sin and death in the millennium (Isa. 65:20; Rev. 20:7-8). Following one last rebellious uprising toward the end of Jesus' thousand-year reign in Jerusalem, God will put a final end to sin and death, ushering in eternity future. Therefore, we see the Millennial Kingdom sandwiched between two major end-times events: the second coming of Jesus, and the beginning of eternity future.

WHERE WILL THE MILLENNIAL KINGDOM BE LOCATED?

In the previous chapter on Zechariah 14, we discussed the devastating siege of Jerusalem that Jesus swiftly puts to an end at His second coming. This chapter in Zechariah provides several key details about the location of Jesus' future kingdom.

To recap, after Jesus descends on the Mount of Olives and defeats the nations gathered against Jerusalem, the city will become the capital of the Millennial Kingdom and the residence of the King. The temple will be restored (Ezek. 40–48). The surrounding topography will be completely changed so Jerusalem stands on the highest hill in the area (Zech. 14:10). Living water will flow from Jerusalem west toward the Mediterranean and east toward the Dead Sea, transforming the Dead Sea into a body of fresh, life-giving water (Ezek. 47:8).

There will still be distinct nations in the Messianic Age, including Egypt (Zech. 14:18-19). But what about Israel? We learn in the book of Isaiah that Israel will not only continue to exist as a nation in the Messianic Kingdom, but the borders of the land will be drawn according to God's land grant to Abraham in Genesis 15.

> On that day
> the LORD will thresh grain from the Euphrates River
> as far as the Wadi of Egypt,
> and you Israelites will be gathered one by one.
> On that day
> a great ram's horn will be blown,
> and those lost in the land of Assyria will come,
> as well as those dispersed in the land of Egypt;
> and they will worship the LORD
> at Jerusalem on the holy mountain. (Isa. 27:12-13)

Compare this to what Moses wrote in Genesis centuries earlier: "On that day the LORD made a covenant with Abram, saying, "I give this land to your offspring, from the Brook of Egypt to the great river, the Euphrates River" (Gen. 15:18). Under the Messiah's reign, Israel will finally possess the borders of the land

God had promised to Abraham, and it will belong to them *min olam v'ad olam*—forever and ever.

What Will Life Be Like in the Millennial Kingdom?

In this section, we will look at three passages of Scripture that give us a glimpse into the lifestyle of those residing in the Millennial Kingdom. In Isaiah 65:19-21, the prophet describes Jesus' future kingdom as one in which God's relationship with His people has been restored, longevity is the norm, and those who work enjoy the fruits of their labor. This stands in contrast to the brokenness, premature death, and injustice we see throughout the world today.

Additionally, Isaiah 11:6-9 paints a picture of the incredible harmony that will prevail in the natural world during Jesus' millennial reign. Predatory animals like wolves, leopards, bears, and lions will dwell peacefully alongside lambs, goats, and cows (vv. 6-7). Not only that, but "an infant will play beside the cobra's pit, and a toddler will put his hand into a snake's den" (v. 8). Any responsible parent would be horrified to find their young child in this situation today, but in the future there will be no need to fear, "for the land will be as full of the knowledge of the Lord as the sea is filled with water" (v. 9). The harmony that pervades the Millennial Kingdom will apply to the relationship between people and animals as well.

Along with the blessings of longevity, fruitfulness, and universal peace, another vital aspect of life in the Millennial Kingdom is the yearly pilgrimage everyone makes to Jerusalem to pay homage to the King and celebrate Sukkot, the Feast of Booths. Anyone who refuses to make this annual trip will experience drought as a consequence of their disobedience. This yearly celebration of Sukkot in the Millennial Kingdom is recorded in Zechariah 14.

In spite of the amazing improvements and restoration that will take place in the millennium, there will nonetheless be the ongoing presence of sin. Even though the average human lifespan will increase, death will remain a reality (Is. 65:20). The nations can still choose to disobey God, and suffering will still result from God's just discipline (Zech. 14:17-19). There is a distinction between the Millennial Kingdom and eternity future, where "death will be no more; grief, crying, and pain will be no more, because the previous things have passed away" (Rev. 21:4).

WHO WILL BE PRESENT IN THE MILLENNIAL KINGDOM?

It is clear that the righteous in God's eyes, both those who lived before and after Messiah's first coming, are present in the future Millennial Kingdom. We know Old Testament saints will inhabit the Messianic Kingdom together with New Testament saints because the promises of a future kingdom were first given to Abraham and his descendants (Gen. 15; Isa. 2:1-4; 11:6-9; 65:17-25). If God excluded Old Testament saints from the kingdom, He would be breaking this promise to Abraham.

In addition to the righteous who lived before the coming of the Messiah, New Testament saints are promised they will rule and reign with the Messiah (Rev. 5:10). Although the kingdom age is going to be glorious in many respects, it will not be perfect. As will be discussed below, death is still present, and Revelation 20:8 teaches that a great number of people will be deceived by Satan at the conclusion of the millennium. So, if the righteous are present in their resurrected, imperishable bodies, who are the people who die? In addition, who are the people being deceived by Satan at the end of the Messianic Age?

To answer these questions, we need to revisit the end of the seven-year Tribulation Period, when God's wrath will be poured out on the earth. There will be many people who die during the Tribulation, but there will also be survivors. Although many people will refuse to believe, many others will find salvation in Jesus. Some of these believers will be martyred, but others will endure until the end of the Tribulation and be welcomed into the future kingdom. However, these surviving believers will still be in their natural bodies, so they will need to experience a bodily death in order to receive their resurrected bodies.

This means a situation exists at the beginning of the kingdom where believers, in their natural bodies, are living alongside believers in their resurrected bodies. We read about a similar situation in the Gospels when Jesus, in His resurrected body, encounters and interacts with those still in natural bodies (Luke 24:13-53). As time goes by in the Millennial Kingdom, the descendants of those believers who survived the Tribulation will likewise have natural bodies.

By the end of the Messianic Age, it is likely there will be millions of these descendants, and they will each need to make the personal decision to put their faith in Jesus. Unfortunately, even though the kingdom is a glorious place with the Messiah reigning on the throne in Jerusalem, some born in this unique time will still choose unbelief. Many unbelievers will be deceived by Satan at the end of the era and follow him into rebellion. John describes the outcome of this rebellion in Revelation 20:9-10:

> They [the deceived nations] came up across the breadth of the earth and surrounded the encampment of the saints, the beloved city. Then fire came down from heaven and consumed them. The devil who deceived them was thrown into the lake of fire and sulfur where the beast and the false prophet are, and they will be tormented day and night forever and ever.

HOW LONG WILL THE MILLENNIAL KINGDOM LAST?

In Revelation 20, the duration of the Millennial Kingdom is explicitly stated as one thousand years. In fact, we find this length repeated six times in just seven verses. The events of Revelation 20 occur at the end of the Tribulation Period, when Jesus returns as a mighty warrior and defeats the armies of the antichrist. The beast (who represents the antichrist) and the false prophet are captured and thrown into the lake of fire (Rev. 19:19-21). After this,

> I [John] saw an angel coming down from heaven holding the key to the abyss and a great chain in his hand. He seized the dragon, that ancient serpent who is the devil and Satan, and bound him for a thousand years. He threw him into the abyss, closed it, and put a seal on it so that he would no longer deceive the nations until the thousand years were completed. After that, he must be released for a short time. (Rev. 20:1-3)

One of the reasons the Millennial Kingdom will be such a time of unprecedented peace and goodness is the imprisonment of Satan in the abyss. The adversary's temporary confinement will prevent him from "prowling around like a roaring lion, looking for anyone he can devour" (1 Peter 5:8). Satan is still actively deceiving the nations today, but he will be powerless to do so during Jesus' millennial reign.

The future binding of Satan poses a major problem for the amillennial view. If we already live in the kingdom, where Satan has been locked away, how can the continued presence of overwhelming satanic influence in our world be explained? It is far more plausible that Satan is currently still allowed to exercise his evil power over the nations; the one thousand years of Jesus' reign and Satan's imprisonment are still future.

The length of the Millennial Kingdom appears several other times in John's account. In the future kingdom, the resurrected saints, including those who were martyred during the Tribulation Period for their faith, will reign with Jesus for one thousand years (Rev. 20:4, 6). At the end of the thousand years, Satan will be released briefly from the abyss and lead a worldwide rebellion against the Messiah. Satan's forces will surround the saints dwelling in Jerusalem, but they will be consumed by fire from heaven (vv. 7-9). Following this massive failed revolt, the remaining dead will be raised to life at the end of the thousand years, to be judged before God's throne (vv. 5, 11-15).

Some interpreters believe that the number 1,000 in these verses, instead of a literal millennium, just means a very long period of time that isn't necessarily fixed. However, a figurative interpretation of the number 1,000 in Revelation 20 is inconsistent with how we interpret the rest of the numbers in the book.

For example, consider the seven churches mentioned in Revelation 2–3. Rarely would anyone argue that these were not seven literal, historical churches. The same principle applies to the seven lampstands, the four living creatures, the twenty-four elders, the seven seals, the seven trumpets, the two witnesses, and the 144,000 sealed from the tribes of Israel. In Revelation 7:4-8, John divides the 144,000 Israelites into 12,000 from each of the twelve tribes. This precise breakdown would be meaningless if the numbers were figurative. If we accept the other numerical values in Revelation at face value, we should also interpret the future reign of Jesus literally as lasting for one thousand years.

CONCLUSION

In the future, after Jesus' second coming, He will set up a literal kingdom on earth and reign with His saints for one thousand years. This Millennial Kingdom is a prominent topic in Scripture and was of concern to the prophets, the disciples, and Jesus himself. It is a future dominion located on earth, with Jerusalem as its capital and the seat of the Messiah's reign. Life in this kingdom will be characterized by longevity and fruitfulness, which stem from a restored relationship with God. There will be widespread peace and reverent worship of the messianic King. The Millennial Kingdom will last for one thousand years, after which Satan and all of his followers will be cast into the lake of fire. Only after all of these things have been accomplished will eternity begin, when God will make all things new (Rev. 21:1-5).

Paul defined the current reality for every believer when he wrote, "He [God] has rescued us from the domain of darkness and transferred us into the kingdom of the Son he loves. In him we have redemption, the forgiveness of sins" (Col. 1:13-14). Though the Messianic Kingdom has not yet arrived, the task before each believer is to live as kingdom citizens in the present. We will expand on how the Bible instructs us to live as citizens of Jesus' kingdom in the afterword.

> *Listen to the first episode of the five-part series on The TŌV Podcast, "Demystifying the Millennial Kingdom: the Evidence."*

> *Or you can watch this series on our YouTube channel*

Afterword

Congratulations! You've worked your way through eight chapters of solid biblical teaching on Israel in prophecy. Perhaps this was your first time thinking through some of the material on this subject. Or perhaps you are an "eschatology maven" with expertise in prophetic Scripture. Most believers likely find themselves somewhere in between. Regardless, we all have more to glean from the Word of God.

Beyond having the satisfaction of soaking in the Scriptures (and finishing a substantive book), what are your key takeaways? Hopefully, you've confirmed you are building your life on a strong foundation. Levi began in chapter one by reminding us: 1) biblical prophecy is accurate; 2) God's revelation of Israel's (and our) wonderful future provides comforting assurance when our world is in chaos; 3) our worldview is grounded in reality (God's truth); and 4) our hearts are stirred to love and trust God all the more as we see His sovereign plan unfolding toward a glorious climax.

The apostle John gives an additional personal benefit of considering the summation of history:

> Beloved, now we are children of God, and it has not appeared as yet what we will be. We know that when He appears, we will be like Him, because we will see Him just as He is. And everyone who has this hope fixed on Him purifies himself, just as He is pure. (1 John 3:2-3)

Rather than being "so heavenly minded we're of no earthly good," John indicates keeping the end in view will motivate us to live in purity. And, as Levi has noted, this should be a natural outgrowth of our increased love for the Lord, and not mere outward compliance with a set of external rules. Salvation is a gift we don't merit (Eph. 2:8-9; Titus 3:5-6), and having been "born from above" by faith (John 3:3), we don't strive to keep ourselves saved or impress God by good works.

In John's words, the key to righteous living is having "this hope fixed on Him." Or as the writer of Hebrews states it, "fixing our eyes on Jesus, the author and perfecter of faith" (12:2). One day we will be like Jesus. Beyond anything we could have asked or imagined, we are being transformed into the very image of the Son of God!

In Romans 8:29-30, Paul details the process: "For those whom He foreknew, He also predestined to become conformed to the image of His Son, so that He would be the firstborn among many brethren; and these whom He predestined, He also called; and these whom He called, He also justified; and these whom He justified, He also glorified."

And we may be "confident of this very thing, that He who began a good work in you will perfect it until the day of Messiah Jesus" (Phil. 1:6). In God's sight, we are already seated with Messiah "in the heavenly places" (Eph. 2:6).

But until we physically enter the world to come, we have to navigate in this one. Knowing what lies ahead, how should believers prioritize the time that remains?

We explore this question in the episode "Navigating This Life" on The TŌV Podcast.

At Life in Messiah, we have as our highest aim to "please the Audience of One." God's glory and smile of approval are what we seek above all else. We recognize that "trying harder to do better" in our own strength and wisdom will never accomplish what God purposes for us to be and do.

So we remind ourselves "there is no substitute for being controlled by the Holy Spirit." The Spirit was our Savior's "parting gift" to His disciples. Jesus would no longer be with them; far better, He said at the Last Supper, was that His Spirit would dwell in them—and in all who place their trust in Him.

The beauty of being Spirit-filled means we have the guidance to know what God designs for our daily walk. He changes us by renewing our minds so we desire to do what He desires. And the Holy Spirit produces the fruit that demonstrates the genuineness of our faith: love, joy, peace, patience, kindness, goodness, faithfulness, gentleness, and self-control (Gal. 5:22-23).

God has sovereign control over the events of history which will culminate in a glorious summing up of all things in Messiah in the fullness of time (Eph. 1:10). So, does the fact that Jesus has accomplished our redemption mean we simply lounge around waiting for the assured conclusion?

Hardly! While we don't work *for* our salvation, we are to work *out* our salvation, with holy awe of Whom we serve. But we rely on the reality that "it is God who is at work in you, both to will and to work for His good pleasure" (Phil. 2:13). We are "created in Messiah Jesus for good works, which God prepared beforehand so that we would walk in them" (Eph. 2:10).

Here are five examples of what we at Life in Messiah ask the Lord to help us with as we desire His will to be done on earth as it is in heaven.

1. Walk in humility, faith, and obedience. We begin with humility—the recognition that we are dependent creatures in whose flesh dwells no good thing. We continue to surrender our wills to His, asking the Spirit to help us hear clearly and heed quickly when He prompts. "Lord, you have my 'Yes'; now what would You have me do?"

We were saved by grace through faith; Scripture enjoins us to walk by faith and not by sight. When we realize our human limitations and recognize the all-sufficiency of our omniscient, omnipotent God, it is easier to rely upon Him, in all matters of life.

If we get the humility and faith elements right, obedience readily follows. But how do we know His will for daily life?

2. Read the Bible daily. We don't get emails from heaven. Most of us won't experience angelic visitations. But God does speak to us through His Word. Though we find plenty of historical data and prophetic predictions in Scripture, the Bible does far more than impart information. God's very character, including His love for His people, is on full display. If you want to love the God of the Word more, get better acquainted with the Word of God.

Daily disciplines are a great idea. Old habits aren't easily broken nor new ones easily formed. But many will testify that getting started with even a little time in God's Word with regularity is a great way to develop an appetite for more.

Serious Bible students have access to an overwhelming amount of external helps, many of which are available at our fingertips electronically. Personally, some of my richest time in the Word has been spent with a box of colored pencils used to highlight or underline various aspects of Scripture in my old-fashioned printed Bible. For example, promises are colored green; sin, judgment, and death are dark gray. Prophetic passages are underlined in green ink. So when I have a green-underlined verse colored in gray, I'm looking at a prophetic utterance with impending judgment. Instructions, commands, and exhortations are dark blue. Principles, salvation, positive and negative testimonies each have a different color. And because Israel has a unique role in God's plan, I highlight those passages in brown.

A series of symbols are helpful margin notations. For example, a water drop is placed next to verses about baptism; the Holy Spirit is represented by a flame. This technique not only made me a better student of the Word, it also helped me teach without notes, keeping me grounded in the text. What have you found helpful as you meditate on Scripture?

3. Develop a habit of prayer. If prayer is viewed merely as ritual, rote, or requirement, we're missing the point. Prayer is communion with our loving Creator. He delights in our worship; He inhabits the praises of His people (Ps. 22:3).

God invites us to cast our cares upon Him because He cares for us (1 Peter 5:7). He delights to give good gifts to His children (Matt. 7:11), but reminds us we have not because we ask not, or because we ask selfishly (James 4:2-3).

Praying "without ceasing" (1 Thess. 5:17) means actively including the Lord in the events of daily life, having a sense of His presence. He has promised to never leave or forsake us (Heb. 13:5) and is a friend who sticks closer than a brother (Prov. 18:24). So why not commune with Him, when He invites us to?

Jesus not only modeled prayer for us while on earth, He makes intercession for us in heaven (Heb. 7:25). And when we're too exhausted, confused, or under attack to pray clearly, the Spirit Himself intercedes for us (Rom. 8:26-27). How about that? We have divine "prayer partners" who pray for us when we cannot!

4. Love others well, including the Jewish people! In the Upper Room, Jesus issued a new commandment: "love one another."[35] But how is this a new commandment—and what distinguishes it from "the greatest commandments" to 1) love God; and 2) love our neighbors as ourselves?

The difference is found in how Jesus concludes the new commandment: "as I have loved you." No longer is the measure of love internal (as I love myself) but external (as Jesus loved us and gave Himself for us). That is an unattainable standard, unless God's love is poured out through me. That happens as "Messiah lives in me" through His Spirit who produces the fruit of love (Gal. 2:20).

"We love, because He first loved us" (1 John 4:19). We know what love looks like, because Jesus modeled it. "Greater love has no one than this, that one lay down his life for his friends" (John 15:13).

And we know the early church caught the message. Peter twice echoes "love one another" in his first epistle; John and Paul each repeat it five times—for a total of twelve. Paul describes how love behaves (not feels) in 1 Corinthians 13.

And if we want a "scorecard" to know how we're doing, the New Testament writers provide twenty-two positive

---

35   In fact, Jesus mentions love 31 times in His final instructions before His crucifixion. Four of those times He says, "Love one another" (twice in John 13:34; 15:12, 17). That love is a major theme in John's writings is clearly seen in a simple word count: Gospel of John – 57; 1 John – 46; 2 John – 4; 3 John – 3; and Revelation – 7. That's 117 times that *agape* (101) and *phileo* (16) appear in John's writings alone.

reciprocal ("one another") commands.[36] Nine negative actions are identified that we should avoid doing to one another.[37]

And why do we add "especially the Jewish people" to the Lord's command to love? At Life in Messiah, our mission statement is "Sharing God's heart for the Jewish people." We believe God indeed has a special love for the offspring of Jacob. We believe it because He says so.

In Deuteronomy 7:6-8, God specifies His reasons for choosing Israel as His own special possession: His love and His promises to the patriarchs. He further states, "I have loved you [Israel] with an everlasting love; therefore, I have drawn you with lovingkindness" (Jer. 31:3).

As Levi has demonstrated through this book, God is not finished with Israel! His covenant faithfulness to His promises and His enduring love for His chosen nation remain intact.[38]

We can't rewrite the history of the last two millennia. But we can make a difference in our generation! What would it look like for the Jewish people in your sphere of influence to have Messiah's love demonstrated to them in personal, practical

36   Of these, the generic "love one another" is cited sixteen times. "Be like minded toward," "bear with," "build up," "encourage," forgive," "give preference to," "serve," and "speak to/admonish" are found twice each; all others have one use except "greet one another," which has four. Two additional "state of being" statements (not counted above) are also found: "we are members of one another" (Eph 4:25) and "have fellowship with one another" (1 John 1:7).

37   Each of these "reciprocal don'ts" are found once: challenge, complain against, deprive maritally, devour, envy, judge, lie to, speak against, and sue.

38   Those who believe God can abandon His people because of their waywardness would do well to read God's review of Jewish history in Ezekiel 20. God details Israel's recurring unbelief and idolatry, and acknowledges He has good reason to abandon them. But He concludes His history lesson with a promise of future restoration—all for His name's sake!

ways? As antisemitism increases globally and hatred of Israel grows exponentially, the love Christians display stands in stark contrast. We pray you will be an instrument of God's love to the Jewish people you encounter—for His name's sake.

5. Share the gospel. Nothing demonstrates love more than caring for the betterment of others. For too many people over the centuries, the Jewish people have been objects of scorn and derision if not persecution, expulsion, and extermination. "No one cares for my soul," in the words of the psalmist (Ps. 142:4), is the lament of many Jewish people.

But God says, "'For I will restore you to health and I will heal you of your wounds,' declares the LORD, 'because they have called you an outcast, saying: "It is Zion; no one cares for her"'" (Jer. 30:17).

That's a promise of future restoration, and perhaps that day is drawing very near. But what about today? God has a faithful remnant among the Jewish people in every generation.[39] Paul gives God's blueprint for the church in Ephesians 2: of the two people groups (Jews and Gentiles) He is making one new man (vv. 11-22).

So, based on God's promises and His stated purpose, we can confidently be assured He will add Jewish believers to Messiah's body in every generation—ours included. How we rejoice to see that number growing with each passing year!

If you're not sharing the gospel with Jewish people, why not? If it's because you don't live in a community with Jewish people, you can still pray for their spiritual eyes to be opened

---

39   For example, God references the seven thousand who have not bowed the knee to Baal in 1 Kings 19:18. See also Romans 11:3-5.

to the truth of the gospel. And if you're connected to the internet, you can find Jewish people to interact with online.

If you're not sure how to sensitively begin a gospel presentation or effectively present the best-ever news of salvation in a Jewish context, we'd love to help! Our outreach website www.insearchofshalom.com has some helpful resources. *Reaching Jewish People for Messiah* is our primer to get you started. Contact us at www.lifeinmessiah.org or call 708-418-0020 and let us know how we can best be of help to you in sharing God's heart for the Jewish people.

Because Israel and the Jewish people matter to God, they should matter to us.

WES TABER
Life in Messiah Global Ambassador

Scan here to get a free ebook copy of the book "Reaching Jewish People for Messiah."

Made in the USA
Columbia, SC
15 September 2024

41837701R00059